S0-BQS-063

CLIMATE
ACTION

made possible by a generous grant from
THE WILLIAM AND FLORA HEWLETT FOUNDATION

Editors-in-Chief Deborah Chasman & Joshua Cohen

Managing Editor and Arts Editor Adam McGee

Senior Editor Matt Lord

Engagement Editor Rosie Gillies

Manuscript and Production Editor Hannah Liberman

Contributing Editors Junot Díaz, Adom Getachew, Walter Johnson, Amy Kapczynski, Robin D.G. Kelley, Lenore Palladino

Contributing Arts Editor Ed Pavlić

Editorial Assistant Meghana Mysore

Marketing and Development Manager Dan Manchon

Special Projects Manager María Clara Cobo

Finance Manager Anthony DeMusis III

Printer Sheridan PA

Board of Advisors Derek Schrier (chair), Archon Fung, Deborah Fung, Alexandra Robert Gordon, Richard M. Locke, Jeff Mayersohn, Jennifer Moses, Scott Nielsen, Robert Pollin, Rob Reich, Hiram Samel, Kim Malone Scott

Interior Graphic Design Zak Jensen & Alex Camlin

Cover Design Alex Camlin

Climate Action is *Boston Review* Forum 16 (45.4)

To become a member, visit bostonreview.net/membership/

For questions about donations and major gifts, contact Dan Manchon, dan@bostonreview.net

For questions about memberships, call 877-406-2443 or email Customer_Service@bostonreview.info.

Boston Review
PO Box 390568
Cambridge, MA 02139-0568

ISSN: 0734-2306 / ISBN: 978-1-946511-67-6

CONTENTS

EDITORS' NOTE
Joshua Cohen & Deborah Chasman

THE CALAMITIES OF CLIMATE CHANGE are with us, as temperatures continue to reach record highs and unprecedented disasters ravage the globe, from historic wildfires in the western United States to dwindling ice sheets in the Arctic. Despite the damage—not to mention decades of activism and longstanding scientific consensus— our economies remain deeply dependent on fossil fuels. What has impeded progress on deep decarbonization of the economy? And how are we to meet the challenge of warming before it is too late? *Climate Action* aims to answer these fundamental questions.

Leading off a forum, Charles Sabel and David G. Victor explain why global climate change diplomacy—which has monopolized policy thinking for decades—has failed to deliver significant results. Instead, they argue, we must embrace what they call "experimentalist governance." Taking inspiration from the pragmatist philosophy of John Dewey as well as from the Montreal Protocol's successful approach to ozone depletion, they argue for an architecture that promises to integrate bottom-up local experimentation with top-down global cooperation.

Respondents consider how that program might work in practice, where it fits alongside plans for a Green New Deal, and, perhaps most importantly, whether it can have the political impact needed to repair the damage.

Other contributors to *Climate Action* explore the limitations of carbon pricing, the prospects of recent corporate commitments to rein in emissions, and the nature of life on a polluted and overheated planet. Together they sketch an urgent and ambitious vision for climate action—now.

FORUM

HOW TO FIX THE CLIMATE

Charles Sabel
& David G. Victor

CAN THE WORLD meet the challenge of climate change? After more than three decades of global negotiations, the prognosis looks bleak. The most ambitious diplomatic efforts have focused on a series of virtually global agreements such as the Kyoto Protocol of 1997 and the Paris Agreement of 2015. With so many diverse interests across so many countries, it has been hard to get global agreement simply on the need for action; *meaningful* consensus has been even more elusive. Profound uncertainty about the effectiveness of various mitigation measures has made it difficult to estimate the cost of deep cuts in emissions.

What is certain is that cuts will pose a threat to well-organized, high-emitting industries. Prudent negotiators have delayed making commitments and agreed only to treaties that continue business as usual by a more palatable name. Between the delays and superficial compacts, emissions have risen by two-thirds since 1990, and they keep climbing—except for the temporary drop this year when the global economy imploded under the coronavirus pandemic. To stop the rise in global temperature, emissions must be cut deeply—essentially to zero over the long term.

Meanwhile, it is getting harder to agree on collective responses to any urgent global question. The expansion of trade and the diffusion of new technologies have undermined U.S. geopolitical dominance and accelerated the rise of China and the Global South while producing a surge in inequality and open mistrust of elites. The World Trade Organization (WTO), founded in 1995, has been paralyzed for more than a decade by the kind of consensus decision-making that hamstrung climate diplomacy. In many other domains, from human rights to investment to monetary coordination, order seems to be fraying. With no global hegemon and no trusted technocracy—welcome changes in the eyes of many—there is no global authority to mend it.

Popular protest has reinforced this global gridlock. The Great Recession of 2008 exposed the limits of the postwar model of economic growth and revealed the growing divide between those who stand to benefit from rapid innovation and expanding trade and those who, often with good reason, fear both. The economic shock triggered this year by the pandemic dramatically underscored and exacerbated those divisions. No wonder that fears and hopes about economic revival and responses to climate change, already tightly linked, have in recent years become densely intertwined politically.

For conservatives in many countries, decarbonization is a fraught symbol of the elite, and repudiating climate agreements—including Trump's snubbing of the Paris Agreement—is a way to reassert the primacy of national interests after decades of unchecked globalism. For progressives, meanwhile, the need to reconcile sustainability and inclusive well-being finds expression in calls for massive public investments such as the Green New Deal. That vision has found tentative success in only a small fraction of the global economy, one that accounts for a small and shrinking slice of global emissions.

But this record, bleak as it is, is not the whole story. Alongside the string of make-believe global climate agreements and false visions of sure-fire solutions are significant and promising successes in many other domains—and we can learn from them in the fight to rein in warming. Consider just three examples.

First, the Montreal Protocol, an international treaty first crafted in 1987, has put the planet on the path to eliminate gases that destroy the ozone layer and themselves often contribute to warming.

Second, the California Air Resources Board (CARB), founded in the late 1960s to respond to smog choking Los Angeles, works in rough concert with car companies and the makers of pollution-control devices to tighten standards for vehicular emissions without imposing unworkable goals along the way. CARB and other California regulatory agencies have accelerated development of the electric car and other innovations, demonstrating that even in the United States regulation can push technology in the direction of public interest. Together these policies anticipate key elements of a green industrial policy.

Third, the Water Framework Directive (WFD) of the European Union induced extensive experimentation with new forms of river-basin and watershed governance that, twenty years after passage of the law, are connecting national, regional, and ground-level decision-making to make tangible progress on one of the most vexing water pollution problems—the runoff of agrochemicals and animal wastes from farms.

From the global to the local levels, then—and at every level in between—models of effective problem-solving have already emerged and continue to make progress on issues that, like climate change, are marked by a diffuse commitment to action but no clear plan for how to proceed. These efforts work in countries as diverse as China and Peru, and for international problems as diverse as protecting the ozone layer and cutting marine pollution. They address challenges as intrusive and contentious as any that arise with deep decarbonization, and they tackle challenges for which solutions require unseating powerful interests and transforming whole industries.

These efforts work by acknowledging up front the likelihood of false starts and overreach, given the fact that the best course of action is unknowable at the outset. They encourage ground-level initiative by creating incentives for actors with detailed knowledge of mitigation problems to innovate, then convert the solutions into standards for all. But they also enable ground-level participation in decision-making to ensure that general measures are accountably contextualized to local needs. When experiments succeed, they provide the information and practical examples needed to mold politics and investment differently —away from vested interests and toward clean development.

Sabel & Victor

We call this approach to climate change cooperation *experimentalist governance*. It is sharply at odds with most diplomatic efforts that have so far failed to make much of a dent in global warming. Since climate change is by nature a global problem, the architects of global climate treaties assume that solutions also have to be global *from the start*. Since cutting emissions is costly, and each nation is tempted to shirk its responsibilities and shift the costs to others, climate diplomats assume that no one will cooperate unless all are bound by the same commitments. From those assumptions come the requirement that climate change agreements be global in scope and legally binding. At the same time, the United Nations General Assembly—the legal body that authorized in 1990 what became the UN Framework Convention on Climate Change (UNFCCC), the parent to every global climate agreement since—asserted that no climate agreement should intrude on any nation's sovereignty. By this logic, the UNFCCC requires binding consensus among all sovereign members—a global compact that allows formal global choices no more ambitious than what the least ambitious will allow.

But what if, extrapolating from the examples above, the only practical way to get to a workable global solution is to encourage and piece together partial ones? What if the best way to build an effective consensus is not to ask who will commit to achieving certain outcomes no matter what, but instead by inviting parties to start by solving problems at many scales? And what if rewards and sanctions were designed to make it risky for reluctant innovators not to join in when mitigation efforts begin—and then, when advances are consolidated, very costly for less capable actors to delay improvements that are demonstrably feasible?

In short, what if a global approach with binding commitments could and should be the outcome of our efforts, not the starting point?

An Exemplary Success

TO GET A FIX on what an experimentalist approach to governance might mean, concretely, for limiting global warming, consider again the Montreal Protocol, by many measures the single most effective agreement on international environmental protection. It demonstrates that it is possible to catalyze and then speed the broad diffusion of the kinds of innovation in products and production processes needed to alter industries, albeit at a scale much more modest than the disruption implicated with deep decarbonization.

Crafted in the late 1980s, the protocol was ahead of its time. Then and now, everyone agreed that Montreal was effective in protecting the ozone layer, but the reasons for its success were misunderstood by those who immediately used Montreal as the model for climate change diplomacy in the 1990s. The UNFCCC was created in its image without adopting any of the machinery—especially the sector-based systems for advancing innovation—that explain why Montreal worked. Montreal's central place in both the old, ineffective world of climate change diplomacy and its exemplary role in the emerging one of experimentalist governance makes it a good vantage point from which to look ahead to an institutional architecture that takes uncertainty for granted—making it a spur to innovation rather than a cause of gridlock.

Beginning in the 1970s, scientists detected chemical reactions thinning the atmospheric ozone layer that protects most life on Earth from ultraviolet radiation. The cause was traced to emissions of chlorofluorocarbons (and later other chemicals, including halons) that were then widely used in the manufacture of many products, from aerosol sprays to fire extinguishers, styrofoam, refrigeration and industrial lubricants, and cleaning solvents. After more than a decade of contentious debate, two linked treaties, the Vienna Convention (1985) and the Montreal Protocol (1987), created the framework for a global regime, for which governance procedures were elaborated in the following years.

The core of this vision is a schedule to control and eventually eliminate nearly all ozone-depleting substances (ODS). The measures are reassessed every few years in light of current scientific, environmental, technical, and economic information, and the schedule was adapted as necessary. The periodic meeting of the parties has broad authority to review implementation of the overall agreement, and to make formal decisions to add controlled substances or adjust schedules.

Problem-solving in the regime is broken down into sectors that implicate similar technologies—solvents, plastic foams, refrigerants, halon fire-extinguishing agents, crop fumigants—and guided by committees representing industry, academia, and government regulators. The committees organize working groups of ODS users and producers to review and assess efforts, mainly in industry, to find acceptable alternatives. The reviews look at key individual components as well as whole systems—for example, assessing whether a refrigerant that depletes the ozone layer can be replaced by an analogous and more benign alternative, as well as whether refrigeration systems that utilize these new chemicals can work reliably and at acceptable cost. Pilot projects yield promising leads that attract further experimentation at larger scale, allowing the committees to judge if the nascent solution is robust enough for general use.

If this search comes up short, the committees and their oversight bodies authorize exemptions for "essential" and "critical" uses or extend timetables for phaseout. When the use of ODS was phased out in the metered dose inhalers (MDIs) that propel medication into the lungs of asthmatics, for example, the sectoral committee consulted doctors, pharmaceutical companies, and device manufacturers country by country to determine substitutes and transition schedules that met the safety and efficacy requirements of patients. When firms invented an array of alternative MDIs using benign propellants, the committees put the industry on notice that the old methods would be banned. Innovative firms had a strong incentive not to be left out and persistent laggards faced exclusion from the market.

Over time, an amendment procedure allowed additions within the existing categories of coverage and also brought new categories of emissions under control. The boundaries around "sector" were adjusted as the properties of each class of ODS was understood and as new sectors were implicated.

Membership in the Montreal Protocol expanded sharply as well. Initially the protocol focused on industrialized countries, as they had the highest consumption of ODS and were most compelled politically to stop ozone thinning. But use increased rapidly among developing countries, and to encourage their participation in the protocol, they were allowed to extend their compliance schedules. As a further incentive, essentially all costs of compliance for developing countries were paid by a Multilateral Fund financed by rich countries—costs that included not just new technologies but also the local administrative capacity needed to oversee preparation and execution of comprehensive regulatory plans for phasing out production and use of ozone-destroying chemicals sector by sector. Simply making new technology available would not will these benign alternatives into use—local contextualization was essential, and the fund helped build that capacity. Administratively, the fund is probably the best-managed funding mechanism in the history of international environmental governance. Politically, it helped transform the ozone problem from one with guaranteed deadlock—developing countries did not want to bear all these costs themselves—into one that was more practical politically.

The Montreal regime operates against the backdrop of vague but potentially draconian penalties for governments and firms that drag their feet. For the western governments that initiated the regime, such as the United States, those penalties were electoral. (Those were the bygone days when the United States was a reliable leader on global environmental topics.) For the industrial firms that made the noxious substances, the penalties were about brand value and license to operate. DuPont, the most visible of these firms, broke ranks with the rest of the industry to demand a phaseout; destroying the ozone layer was a big liability for a firm that made most of its money in other kinds of chemicals. (It helped that the alternatives might prove more profitable.) Once there was one innovator, it was too costly for others to lag behind. And in countries that actively undermine the Montreal Protocol—Russia at first but others later on, including India and China—the penalties were threats such as trade sanctions from other powerful governments, mainly in the industrialized world, that wanted Montreal to work and also wanted to make sure their home industries would not be undercut by violators overseas.

Designing for Uncertainty

THE FEATURES OF THE MONTREAL APPROACH that make it a good model can be captured in a handful of linked design principles. These principles describe a distinctive cycle of decision-making well suited to domains, including climate change, marked by great complexity and uncertainty.

This approach starts with a thin consensus among an open group of founding participants motivated to act. Precise definition of problems, let alone the best way to respond to them, is unknowable at the outset, but there is enough agreement on how to get started. For its part, the Montreal Protocol was based on an initial agreement that ozone thinning was a problem that must be stopped, and that a first step would require cutting in half the most widely used ODS by 1998. At the time there was no agreement on the magnitude of the risk, the feasibility of finding particular substitutes by certain dates, or even whether 50 percent cuts were the right goal. Consensus thickens with effort, however, and new knowledge demonstrates both what is needed and which actors are capable and trustworthy. Participation is open, in the sense that new actors outside the circle of founders are invited in as their experience and expertise becomes relevant to addressing core problems.

In this scheme, actual problem-solving is devolved to local or frontline actors—those most likely to have the kind of experience and expertise that embodies unanticipated possibility and unsuspected difficulty. Under Montreal, the most essential ground-level work has been technological and performed by industrial enterprises developing and testing new chemicals and equipment along with local regulators who figure out how this equipment will operate in real-world conditions—for example, how MDIs can meet drug safety standards.

This local problem-solving is regularly monitored by a more comprehensive body. In the case of Montreal, assessment panels and sectoral committees periodically take stock of local problem-solving and help codify lessons. Monitoring is typically implemented by peer review: actors with overlapping but distinct areas of expertise and experience evaluate particular projects against others of their kind. The Multilateral Fund monitors projects in developing countries and updates pooled knowledge about what actions cost and whether they work—vital information because, each time Montreal parties adjusted or amended regulatory obligations, they also needed to update the funding plan. These routines help spot and scale successful innovation and make it easier to nip budding failures. Just as initial, broad understanding of problems is corrected by local knowledge, so local choices are corrected in light of related experience elsewhere.

Comprehensive review leads, in turn, to periodic adjustments and redirection of means and ends. From a distance, Montreal looks like a regime that always ratcheted commitments tighter, but viewed close up, it becomes apparent that progress was less linear. Goals were periodically relaxed through exemptions and deadline extensions when problems proved unexpectedly hard. Science helped identify broad goals, but the pace of on-the-ground problem-solving—along with what the parties were willing to spend in the Multilateral Fund and other funding mechanisms—determined compliance deadlines and the timing of additions to the list of regulated substances. Periodically, a centralized assessment panel takes stock of the lessons and offers a plan for how emission controls could be adjusted, the benefits to the ozone layer, and what it would cost.

A distinctive combination of penalties and rewards incentivizes both public and private participation in this type of regime. By rewarding leaders who bet on change, they make it risky for laggard firms and governments to bet against it. This "penalty default," as it is known, destabilizes the status quo: obstruction becomes the riskiest bet of all. And once the logjam of current interests is broken, shifting the question from *whether* change is possible to *how* it can be implemented in diverse conditions, failure to keep pace is viewed more as a symptom of ignorance and incapacity than an expression of selfish cunning. The initial form this feedback effect takes is to call attention to shortfalls and offer assistance, not punish wrongdoing. Only when misbehavior persists, and comes to seem incorrigible, does the reaction become draconian: actors who repeatedly prove unwilling or unable to improve are threatened with expulsion from the community, typically by being excluded from key markets.

These principles are unfamiliar to the worlds of global climate diplomacy and the academics supporting them. But they are not alien to regulators, firms, and NGOs that have stumbled onto ways of working together to solve problems. They have discovered that the only way to move beyond the status quo is to destabilize it and then learn, quickly, to use the daring and imagination that bubble up in the open space to develop better approaches.

Experimentalist Governance Hidden in Plain Sight

TO UNDERSTAND WHY this experience—so familiar to regulators and firms working on ground-level problem-solving—has not translated easily into international efforts, it is helpful to take a closer look at conventional assumptions, rooted in the experience of stable times, that have tended to guide policy choices.

The most consequential of these is the expectation that organizations are either top down or bottom up. Top-down organizations are bureaucracies of the kind we associate with big corporations or big government. Precise goals are set at the top and translated into detailed rules or operating routines to direct execution. Frontline workers apply the rules or follow the routines; middle managers see that they do, or make ad hoc adjustments as necessary. Bottom-up organizations, in contrast, seem hardly like organizations at all: they are forms of coordination that emerge as actors—on equal footing, left to themselves, and given enough time to suffer the consequences of their mistakes—eventually master common problems.

Paris was a victim of this top-down, bottom-up dichotomy. The Paris meeting was convened in the recognition that top-down climate organization, culminating in the Kyoto Protocol, had failed. Parties to Paris took that failure to mean one had to embrace bottom up. But the opposite of a failure does not make a success. Bottom-up organization without direction and discipline is merely a recipe for churning and inaction.

By contrast, experimentalist governance is neither top down, like a hierarchy, nor bottom up, like a self-organizing group. It is both, in turn, as lower levels of institutions correct higher ones and vice versa; we might just as well say it is neither. Mindful that climate change actors are too heterogeneous in their interests and capacities for self-organization, it imposes top-down framework goals and penalty defaults to give direction to bottom-up invention. And it provides incentives both to capable potential innovators and to less capable potential laggards to encourage advances that are ultimately workable for all. This combination of seemingly incompatible features makes experimentalist governance especially suited to problems such as climate change that carry a significant degree of uncertainty.

The second and closely related false dichotomy that has crippled progress on climate change is the choice between technocracy and democracy. In this vision, organizations are either hierarchically controlled by technocrats and managers asserting or pretending to expertise, or else they are democratically accountable to their members and other stakeholders. Paris, in this sense, rejected the technocracy of global diplomatic climate summitry in favor of commitment to the workings of domestic politics in member countries.

One of those who saw past this dichotomy was pragmatist philosopher John Dewey. Dewey took uncertainty and change as the dominant problems of political life and the need to adapt institutions to new circumstances as the continuing challenge to democracy. The response, he argued, was to explicitly acknowledge the fallibility of current arrangements and to make concrete problems the trigger to adjustment of methods and the clarification of goals. But he cautioned that collaborative investigation of alternatives can only be effective if it integrates the knowledge of experts and the experience and values of citizens, for it is the citizen who knows best "where [the shoe] pinches, even if the expert shoemaker is the best judge of how the trouble is to be remedied." The broad participation of stakeholders in the Montreal sectoral committees provides a glimpse of how such cooperation can work. As trust in elites frays in our democracies and decarbonization reaches deeper into everyday life, this kind of working collaboration between shoemakers and shod is increasingly important. It is how systems of governance—even at the international level—will earn and retain greater democratic accountability.

Beyond Paris

WHERE DOES THIS LEAVE US? Experimentalist governance provides a set of tested principles to guide construction of regimes that do a good job of managing problems steeped in uncertainty when conventional organizations can't. International diplomacy such as the Paris Agreement does have a role to play, but a considerably smaller one than its enthusiasts think. The agreement itself acknowledged that the UNFCCC had come to a diplomatic dead end on emissions targets and timetables in the Kyoto Protocol. Paris also did away with the distinction, codified in Kyoto as part of the price of maintaining consensus, between developed countries, responsible for financing the costs of decarbonization, and developing counties, which were essentially exempted from all obligations. Paris welcomed local initiative and innovation from all. It lets individual countries set their own commitments—in the agreement's jargon, "nationally determined contributions" (NDCs)—with, in principle, regular adjustments aimed at ratcheting the NDCs tighter.

On its surface, then, the Paris commitment to decentralized reliance on NDCs and periodic reviews would seem to welcome, even embody, experimentation, review, and adjustment. But in reality Paris is hamstrung by its reliance on sovereign NDCs and a "rulebook" that makes impossible the intrusive review and scrutiny needed for any system of governance oriented around adjusting ends and means in light of experience. Information in Paris is organized by country, but one of the central lessons from the Montreal experience is that the real work of running experiments and identifying solutions gets done in sectors and subsectors of the economy. The way forward is instead to work sector by sector, within institutions that have the ability to apply experimentalist governance.

With regard to warming-related emissions, in particular, it is useful to distinguish two types of sectors. The first is comprised of globalized and highly concentrated industries, such as aircraft, steel, cement, auto, gas, and oil, whose products or production methods are subject to international standards. Deep decarbonization in such sectors entails risky and costly innovation at the frontier of technology, often driven by penalty defaults. International cooperation is appealing to firms under these conditions because it allows them to pool knowledge and risks—the Swedish steel maker bets on one radical alternative to current methods, the German another, and periodically they carefully compare notes—and because by demonstrating the feasibility of alternatives they can raise standards and protect themselves against cut-throat competition from firms that continue to produce the traditional way. Thus Maersk, the world's largest container shipping company by fleet size and cargo volume—and thus the firm best positioned to gain from successful advances—coordinated, inside the International Maritime Organization (IMO), a series of technology demonstration programs cofunded with governments and linked to proposals for new standards. Because cargo ships are long-lived and hard to change once built, Maersk also undertakes to work with those same governments to gradually align equipment and local standards to superior solutions, demonstrating the workability of many paths to improvement and making it easier for other IMO members to join in.

At the opposite extreme are sectors such as residential and commercial construction and power grids incorporating clean energy sources. Production is largely for local markets, using many local inputs, even if key components such as wind turbines or nuclear fuel or flooring materials are global commodities; standards are more likely to be local and national than international. Integrating renewables on California's grid is different than doing so on India's, even though both buy solar panels from the same global market. Cooperation can accelerate emissions reductions by pooling learning: even if solutions are quintessentially place-based in this case, they typically result from the re-elaboration of innovative techniques developed elsewhere. Knowing where to start and what doesn't work under conditions similar to one's own are invaluable.

In between are hybrid cases, such as forestry products or palm oil, where inputs are predominantly local but markets—and hence the standards, backed by penalty defaults, controlling access to them—are international. Reducing illegal logging or burning forests to clear land for agriculture requires reaching deep into local economies, often under limited control by the national state, to give small producers lucrative and stable alternatives to the current, environmentally destructive ones. Progress here is slow, but it continues.

Paris can't guide, much less participate directly, in sectoral experimentation at the technological frontier or in the elaboration of place-based solutions. But there has been a profusion of problem-solving efforts on these lines within other forums, often in some measure informed by experimentalist principles. There is, if anything, a surfeit of national and international organizations directed to these tasks. The challenge for international cooperation on climate change isn't creating new sectoral institutions as much as identifying and coordinating the efforts of those that do or could work.

While Paris has little to contribute to this process, it does serve one essential and exclusive function. It is the most legitimate institution in global politics where climate change is discussed; it sets goals that, while probably impossible to meet, are widely agreed as a starting point. Its presence authorizes governments, firms, and NGOs to punish, in the name of Paris, actors that drag their feet. Without Paris it would be much harder for protesters to rattle companies that cause big emissions and push governments to act on climate change. These are the penalty defaults that destabilize the status quo and motivate innovation.

A New Beginning

AS WE WRITE, the United States is still engaged in a momentous election. No matter the ultimate result—whether Democrats take the Senate—we must build institutions for learning under uncertainty as rapidly as possible, for global agreements will not be the engine for change.

The Biden administration will rejoin the Paris Agreement—one of the easiest decisions the new administration will make, and far from the most consequential. After that, things get difficult. Because Washington remains deeply polarized, climate activism will focus on aggressive administrative action—uncomfortably akin, as a matter of administrative law, to some of Trump's expansive uses of executive authority. These actions will seek to increase the pressure on firms in key industries to cut emissions. A further consequence will be redoubling efforts to build place-based solutions outside D.C.—for example, accelerating the ongoing shift to renewables and other zero-emission electric technologies in power grids, where policy and investment decisions are entangled in state politics. The more affordable and reliable these solutions, the easier it will be to overcome tenacious political opposition.

Perhaps the most difficult challenge will be dramatically increasing the resources available to address climate change. We will learn what is possible soon enough. And even if the funding efforts succeed, the question remains whether good intentions will lead to good deeds. There are long lists for big new investments in clean energy (and in many other areas as well), along with flowing plans for regulatory reform—ideas that travel under many names, including the Green New Deal, and are aimed not just at cutting U.S. emissions but also building industries of the green future. Yet these proposals, so far, are strong on mandates and vision and often silent on governance.

It is in connecting ideas to action—and keeping them connected amidst uncertainty—that the lessons of Montreal come to bear. They show how, starting with a thin consensus on goals, experimentalist principles can link innovation at the frontier with on-the-ground problem-solving in a way that greens the economy without asking the impossible of producers or consumers. Paris showed that we could learn, if incompletely, from the failures of orthodox policy to address climate change. It is now long past time to show that we can learn from our unconventional successes as well.

WE NEED POLITICAL—NOT TECHNOLOGICAL—INNOVATION

Alyssa Battistoni

IT IS REFRESHING TO SEE the case against the Paris Agreement made so plainly: for far too long, climate politics has put too many eggs in the basket of global diplomacy, with little to show for it. With their vision of experimentation across different scales of governance, Charles Sabel and David G. Victor lay out a compelling vision of how to move onto more pragmatic ground. Their idea of experimentalist governance promises to open up new models of climate action and change our expectations for what climate progress looks like.

It is concerning, however, that their primary illustration of successful experimentalist governance is the Montreal Protocol. Indeed, the protocol has been held up as a promising model for action on global warming ever since it was ratified in 1987. So why haven't the lessons of Montreal served to advance climate goals in the past three decades?

It should hardly need pointing out that greenhouse gases are significantly different from CFCs in ways that have implications for how they might be phased out. Whereas CFCs were byproducts of a relatively restricted set of goods made by a small number of manufacturers, greenhouse gases are the byproducts of the global economy itself: the world runs on fossil fuels and our ways of living are built around them. Sabel and Victor relegate to a parenthetical the fact that for the major producers of CFCs, newer and less polluting chemicals were more profitable—but this is the real story. Oil and gas companies are among the world's biggest and most powerful, and for them, fossil fuels are not simply one product among many: they are *the* product, and they are wildly profitable. The annual value of CFC production was estimated at $2.2 billion in 1987, while revenue for the oil and gas sector was estimated at $2.5 *trillion* in 2019.

The problem isn't simply that there are differences in context. Rather, Sabel and Victor's proposal too often seems to treat institutional design as a skeleton key to a climate "fix." One is left with the impression that meaningful decarbonization can take place only through technological innovation achieved via the closed-door haggling of regulators and industry. Institutional design does have a role to play, and their analysis of regulatory models offers good ideas for making progress in decarbonizing tricky sectors such as concrete and shipping. But in posing climate change as a problem of "governance" rather than politics, it threatens to fall into the same pitfalls as Paris.

In short, their vision overlooks two essential facts. First, that challenging the power of the fossil fuel industry is the sine qua non of climate politics. And second, that lasting climate action must win popular support.

ON THE FIRST, the limits of Montreal as a model simply can't be divorced from an analysis of the industry in question. The fossil fuel industry knows very well that action on climate poses an existential threat, which is why it has consistently sought to scuttle not only regulation but scientific consensus itself. It has been a notorious funder of climate denial in the United States, but it has also lobbied globally through groups such as the Global Climate Coalition, helping to render global climate agreements unworkable. Why should we expect a sudden good faith to develop solutions? Acknowledgments of "concentrated power" do little to suggest how it might be confronted.

When it comes to democracy, Sabel and Victor invoke Dewey's metaphor of the "shoemakers and the shod" in suggesting a way to integrate the knowledge of experts with the "experience and values" of citizens. But the primary actors in their discussion of experimentalist governance are industries and their regulators—the shod appear only around the margins. In reality, the shoemakers are not friendly neighborhood cobblers or podiatric researchers but multinational conglomerates that act with impunity. Many people's shoes have been pinching for a long time, and they have said so, but no one has paid them much attention. Sabel and Victor have little to say about how trust in elites might be restored.

Indeed, elites play an outsize role in Sabel and Victor's analysis. Yet it is popular movements, from Standing Rock to Sunrise, that have driven climate politics forward and put much more serious climate action on the political agenda. Rather than thinking of the public and its protests as an obstacle to be overcome, we ought to experiment with ways of translating political momentum and bold ideas into concrete projects that decarbonize while also building public support for continued climate action. Sabel and Victor focus primarily on driving *technological* innovation, but *political* innovation will be even more important: figuring out how to deploy technologies we already have to cut carbon as quickly as possible, in ways that build constituencies for further climate action. This is where the Green New Deal comes in.

Sabel and Victor mention the Green New Deal only briefly, as a program for public investment that seems far from becoming reality. It's true that the Green New Deal remains, as yet, a vision without a clear plan for implementation (though there is also a large and growing body of detailed policy work moving in that direction). In the immediate future, it will be crucial to figure out how the ideas animating the Green New Deal can work in practice. Here experimentalist governance has an essential role to play. After all, the original New Deal was itself deeply experimental.

To take one example, California and New Jersey have recently made encouraging commitments to electric vehicle mandates. Better still would be building out robust public transportation systems in order to reduce the need for so many private vehicles in the first place. On this front, experiments are already underway: the city of Lawrence, Massachusetts, made three primary bus routes free to riders last year. Boston is now considering a similar move, thanks to the leadership of city councilor Michelle Wu, who has also just released a Green New Deal plan for the city. Such experiments in accessibility can in turn build on long-standing subsidies for public transportation in countries such as Brazil that have entrenched a constituency for public transit.

Although "green jobs" have been much discussed in climate proposals, in most places there has been no systematic plan to wind down fossil fuel industries and provide a just transition for their workers to move into greener jobs. The current economic crisis presents an excellent opportunity to demonstrate proof of concept. In the United States alone, the drop in oil prices resulting from the global shutdown of economic activity and travel has resulted in an estimated 100,000 lost jobs; around the world, a million fossil fuel jobs are at risk. Why not take the opportunity to experiment with a transitional program that would place fossil fuel industry workers in jobs building green energy infrastructure or doing other decarbonization work, perhaps building off the German model for phasing out coal through a just transition? For that matter, the oil price crash presented a prime opportunity for the state to buy out floundering shale oil producers outright and put them on a path of managed decline. More generally, fossil fuel producers' present vulnerability offers an excellent opportunity to undercut their power.

The Deweyan analogy of shoemakers and shod can come in handy where the energy transition hits the ground with projects seeking to build out clean energy infrastructure at scale. While wind farms, solar arrays, and transmission lines have been blocked by movements of people concerned about the destruction of local landscapes by private developers, democratic procedures that take local concerns seriously and commit to benefits for communities as well as industry could help build support for the expansion of renewables.

Most technological innovation follows the Tesla model: make products for the rich until the cost comes down for everyone else. The Green New Deal for Public Housing Act proposes the opposite: that green design can start with working-class people, tackling the challenges of building retrofits in public housing and developing models that can be used elsewhere. This is the logic of Europe's Energiesprong initiative, now a centerpiece of the proposed Green Deal—to use public subsidy of low-income housing retrofits to cut both emissions and living costs while creating jobs and transforming the overall building sector. The U.S. Department of Energy's Building Technology Office is now working to accelerate the diffusion of that model in the United States.

These proposals for domestic programs are not exhaustive, of course, and will have to adapt to local contexts. But experiments in one part of the world can offer lessons to others. They can also help build the bases for multilateral agreement: countries that have committed to Green New Deal–style programs could form climate clubs committing to use public investment to decarbonize at speed.

THE IDEAS I'VE OUTLINED HERE can start to do three crucial things. First, they can build popular support for action on climate change, developing a counterweight to the fossil fuel industry. Second, they can experiment with ways of living well without the resource-intensive consumption that has characterized our ideas of prosperity to date. And third, they can begin to chart a model of state and economy that can supplant the faltering neoliberal model. Instead of counterposing experiment, public investment, and global agreement, we should seek to align them.

Though such visions may seem politically out of reach, we are now nearly a year into a global crisis that has spurred previously unimaginable forms of state action. You would never know this from Sabel and Victor's proposal, which reads as if it could have been written at any point since 1987. Responses to COVID-19 serve as a reminder that moments of crisis can give rise to radical experimentation. If experimentalist governance is to make good on its promise, it must be able to recognize such extraordinary situations as moments to venture genuinely novel ideas and transformative projects.

THE EXISTENTIAL POLITICS
OF CLIMATE CHANGE
Jessica F. Green

CHARLES SABEL AND DAVID G. VICTOR COUNSEL that we should not despair about the climate crisis. Despite decades of foot-dragging, incremental policies, and increasing emissions, they believe that we can accelerate decarbonization through experimentalist governance. They view climate change largely as a technical problem rather than a political one. With the right institutions, they argue, we can structure learning processes to promote problem-solving.

The authors' optimism is commendable but mistaken. Experimentalist governance puts the cart before the horse. Until governments address the conflicts between the winners and losers of climate change and climate policy, experimentalist governance will be limited in its ambition and impact.

In new work with Thomas Hale and Jeff Colgan, I suggest existential politics as an alternative approach that brings distributional conflicts to the fore. Existential politics is about whose way of life gets to survive. Should we have Miami Beach and the Marshall Islands, or should we have coal miners, ExxonMobil, and Chevron? Some actors will inevitably lose everything—either due to environmental policies or due to the effects of climate change. And both winners and losers will fight like hell to maintain the value of their assets. This obstructionism, not technical problem-solving, is the critical constraint thwarting progress on global climate policy.

In a simplified model of existential politics, the world can be divided into two groups: owners of climate-forcing assets (such as oil and gas firms or heavy industry), and owners of climate-vulnerable assets (such as coastal homeowners and farmers or laborers in climate-vulnerable industries). Ambitious climate policy will devalue—or even destroy—climate-forcing assets (CFAs). Recent news about oil majors' big write downs and Exxon's removal from the Dow Jones Industrial Average has prompted warnings that the end is nigh for the oil industry. While this assertion is debatable, climate policy (as well as the economic downturn resulting from COVID-19) is changing the value of this once indispensable resource. By contrast, NextEra Energy, a utility with a large renewable portfolio, briefly became the most valuable U.S. energy company this month, overshadowing Exxon.

Meanwhile, owners of climate-vulnerable assets (CVAs) face existential threats from the effects of climate change. Perhaps the most dramatic example is that some low-lying island states could completely disappear with sea-level rise. The housing market in Florida, which is particularly vulnerable to rising sea levels, already shows signs of revaluation: both sales and sale prices are falling. The insurance industry, too, is under threat—more extreme weather means bigger payouts. The ongoing 2020 California wildfires have intensified insurance companies' retreat from high-risk areas. If homes are uninsurable, spillover effects will dampen the mortgage market as banks pull back their lending for risky assets. Ripple effects will harm the reinsurance industry, which provides insurance for insurers. As risks intensify, the scale of their spread will too.

Of course, many actors hold both types of assets. Moreover, some will be able to trade one set of assets for another relatively easily, while others will be locked in, shifting both vulnerabilities and, potentially, their political alignments. Typically, holding valuable assets means more power—including greater power to obstruct. CFA owners have historically occupied this role and have been well organized in mobilizing to protect their interests; they have successfully obstructed aggressive climate measures. By contrast, CVA owners tend to be diffuse and less organized. Yet at least some indications suggest that this is changing. Litigation against fossil fuel companies has surged; New York and California have led the charge, seeking compensation for damages incurred due to climate change. Still, we can expect obstructionism—the main obstacle to decarbonization—to again intensify as revaluation ramps up.

IN SUM, while in many cases we do know how to decarbonize, powerful forces are fighting against it. There *are* technical problems that require problem-solving, of course, but they are not the primary constraint on ambitious climate policy. Global climate governance must address politics before policy.

Green

Yet, for Sabel and Victor, politics lurks amorphously in the background, in the form of the penalty default—the incentive or punishment that persuades actors to problem-solve together. In reality, the penalty default is where politics happens. It is shorthand for government intervention—to create incentives for leaders and sanctions for laggards. Yet such intervention requires more than "thin consensus." Governments must be willing and able to legislate.

The cases on which Sabel and Victor ground their optimism had already addressed the fundamental conflicts of existential politics *before* the problem-solving victories that they describe. As David Vogel recounts in *California Greenin'* (2018), the creation of the California Air Resources Board (CARB) occurred against the back-drop of a long-standing fight against air pollution in Los Angeles and, later, across the state. For years prior to CARB's creation, the real estate, agriculture, and tourism industries advocated for more stringent regulations to address smog. Regular "smog attacks" and deaths from smog provoked outrage and public pressure for action. Citizens mobilized a grassroots anti-smog organization. Even the city's most powerful business actor, the Los Angeles Area Chamber of Commerce, pushed for regulation.

Unsurprisingly, the fossil fuel industry initially opposed regulation. However, converging political pressures for regulation, coupled with threats from the *Los Angeles Times* that it would use the publication as a means to publicly shame oil companies, prompted a change of position; oil companies recognized the threat both to their communities and to the long-term viability of their business. Once the obstructionists had reversed course, the technical processes of standard-setting and regulation could proceed in earnest. And when the government of California chose to regulate, it disarmed potential obstruction from the car industry. Largely located outside the state, it had to abide by the new rules or face losing 10 percent of its consumer base.

A similar story applies to the ozone layer. Chlorofluorocarbons (CFCs)—a major ozone-depleting substance—were produced by relatively few firms, which were concentrated in the United States, Japan, the United Kingdom, and France. DuPont was the world's largest producer of CFCs, and while it initially opposed regulation, it had a change of heart when it realized that it could own patents for CFC alternatives and dominate an emerging market. It called for international regulation to ensure that CFC production wasn't simply shifted to unregulated areas (thus undercutting its business), and it turned the threat of asset devaluation into an opportunity by making new, regulation-compatible investments and shifting long-term asset holdings. With this industry support, the U.S. government enthusiastically backed the Montreal Protocol.

Tellingly, the Montreal Protocol has been less successful where political conflicts were not resolved in advance, as is the case with regulation of methyl bromide, another ozone-depleting substance. The chemical was technically phased out in 2005 under the flexible terms of the protocol that Sabel and Victor identify as one of its main strengths. But the U.S. agriculture industry, particularly in California, argued that it would be unable to compete with foreign producers without continued use of methyl bromide. The result was a generous loophole that allows for "critical use exemptions." Though there have been reductions, methyl bromide allotments are still made annually to (mostly developed) countries requesting exemptions. The flexibility of the Montreal Protocol has allowed for adjustments that contravene the primary goal of the treaty, to reduce the production and consumption of ozone-depleting substances.

THESE EXAMPLES ILLUSTRATE that any effective decarbonization policy must confront the reality of asset revaluation and find strategies to address the opposition of those who will lose from climate change and climate policy. Most of this activity will occur on the domestic, rather than the international, level.

Discussions of a just transition away from fossil fuels encapsulate this approach. How do we compensate workers who will be affected by decarbonization policies? Some proposals suggest using workers in the fossil fuel industry to cap abandoned oil and gas wells which leak methane, a powerful greenhouse gas. Others have called for nationalizing the oil industry, which has made minimal progress on decarbonization. In this era of cheap oil, nationalization is a relatively inexpensive proposition: the Next System Project estimates it would cost $550–700 billion in the United States. More generally, industrial policy—governments' investment to promote economic growth—can be used as a tool to compensate CFA owners and empower new coalitions for decarbonization.

More importantly, though, existential politics demands that we expand our understanding of multilateral institutions as engines of ambitious climate policy. Border tax adjustments and carbon tariffs —which would levy carbon taxes on imports based on the carbon emissions they produce—have emerged as serious proposals in the European Union and from President-elect Biden. I have argued for reducing offshore tax shelters as an important element of climate policy. We know that climate change is driven by the world's rich: 1 percent of the population produces more greenhouse gas emissions than the poorest 50 percent. Tax evasion contributes to this problem. The world's wealthiest citizens (the top 0.01 percent) hold roughly 10 percent of world GDP in offshore tax havens. Repatriating these funds would reduce the wealth and the structural power of many CFA owners. In short, we need to think about multilateral cooperation *beyond* the Paris Agreement, looking to the many other multilateral institutions that can help address obstructionism to decarbonization.

Sabel and Victor have the proposals right, but the order wrong. Various sectors *can* do more to overcome specific technological problems and implementation challenges, but only *after* basic material conflicts are resolved. And this will require confronting existential politics.

A DEMOCRATIC GREEN NEW DEAL
Robert C. Hockett

CHARLES SABEL AND DAVID G. VICTOR ARE SPOT ON about the Green New Deal. I can attest to this as someone who helped draft the Green New Deal Resolution, coauthored the accompanying white paper, and developed the Green New Deal finance plan that was commissioned by Representative Alexandria Ocasio-Cortez and which has just been published as a book. What Sabel and Victor say is precisely what we've had in mind all along.

Since it went public early last year, the Green New Deal Resolution has drawn nonstop excitement. And with over 120 U.S. representatives and senators—as well as nearly all of last year's Democratic presidential contenders—signed on, its future looks quite bright. Indeed it looks brighter when you note how much Joe Biden's Build Back Better plan resembles a rebranded Green New Deal.

Accompanying all the excitement of the past eighteen months have been many queries, most of which boil down to a question of how the authors of the Green New Deal Resolution—which is an aspirational, hopeful document—imagine, practically speaking, that its implementation might look. The definitive reply to that is easy: *It's literally up to us.* The Green New Deal Resolution is simply the opening gavel of an extended national deliberation and responsive mobilization—a process meant to include *all of us, right now.*

Two facts about the original New Deal, from which the Green New Deal takes its name, are helpful to remember.

First, the New Deal was never a *done* deal, much less a deal that was done on day one. Rather than a single enactment passed into law early on in a single administration, the New Deal was an organic process—an ongoing project of national recovery and renewal. It unfolded over the course of a decade, and took shape through scores of statutes passed by Congress and signed into law by the president after careful study and long public hearings.

Second, the New Deal had projects in every precinct of the country. All Americans were to benefit, irrespective of political affiliation, vocation, or location. This wasn't only smart politics. *It was democracy.* It was about using the citizenry's commonly owned and operated instrumentality —our federal government—for the benefit of *all* of the citizenry.

This is not to say that the New Deal at all times worked equally well for all Americans. There were flaws in the implementation, owing not only to the spirit of experimentation adopted by the New Dealers, but also to the racism and sexism of the 1930s and '40s. But the point is that the New Deal was meant to be truly national, not simply local or sectional.

Following the New Deal example, this means, first, that the Green New Deal is meant to develop organically over the course of a decade—a decade in which *all* Americans will be proposing, critiquing, and counter-proposing, all in a spirit of joint deliberation about how best to rescue our planet and rejuvenate our economy and society in the process.

Second, it means that we intend, without cavil or qualification, and without shame or embarrassment, for the Green New Deal to *benefit* all Americans. And since Democrats now are less racist and sexist than their Blue Dog predecessors, "all" here means all genders and ethnicities far more than it did in the 1930s and '40s.

How are we acting on this vision? To address this, let me tell you about the Green New Deal Wish List Project, which we've had underway since the summer of 2019.

A challenge confronting newly inaugurated President Barack Obama in 2009 was a lack of shovel-ready projects. This lack meant that even with nearly $1 trillion appropriated for stimulus spending during his first months, Obama had little to spend it on.

We're not letting that happen this time. Working with the same groups that got "the Squad" elected and to which most of us Green New Dealers belong—the Sunrise Movement, Justice Democrats, Democratic Socialists of America, and the like—we are holding town meetings in every town, city, borough, and precinct in the nation. We open each of these the same way: "Imagine," we propose, "that you were told you'd be receiving millions of dollars to spend on whatever projects you think most urgent in making and keeping your town and our planet inhabitable. What would you spend it on? Let's make a list!"

We are assembling these wish lists into binders, county by county and state by state, to deposit with President Biden the day he's sworn in: shovel-ready projects for a bottom-up Green New Deal—its opening move, at any rate.

Of course projects will have to be collated and coordinated; of course the National GND Binder will be a structured synthesis, not a mere heap or aggregation. But all of the substance will nevertheless proceed from countless repeated local town-hall style deliberations.

When she began her orientation as NY-14's new representative in January 2019, Ocasio-Cortez delighted her constituents and many more Americans by posting videos of each day's events on social media. What charmed so many about this was how it included all those who had voted for and otherwise supported the congresswoman in the experience of assuming her responsibilities as their representative. They were there with her, just as assuredly as they'd put her there.

This was participation in government—this was *democracy*—of a kind not unlike when Franklin D. Roosevelt, another avid user of new media, entered "America's living rooms" regularly in his "fireside chats" in the 1930s.

This is precisely how those of us working on the Green New Deal want it to proceed. We want it to develop organically over a decade just as the first New Deal did. We want it to do so *with* the benefit of *all* Americans' wisdom and ideas. And we want it to work *for* the benefit of all of them too. Only in this way will we get our Green New Deal right. Only in this way will it be democratic. And only in this way will it be truly new.

ACHIEVING EQUALITY ON A LIVABLE PLANET
Thea Riofrancos

DESPITE FATALLY SLOW PROGRESS on greening the economy, Charles Sabel and David G. Victor argue that we already have models for effective solutions, even where "intrusive and contentious" challenges arise with deep decarbonization. They are right that such a project requires "unseating powerful interests and transforming whole industries." But with ground-level participation and top-down accountability "contextualized to local needs," they contend, we can steer politics and investment toward clean development.

While this vision of experimentalist governance may find compelling examples in some contexts, it is naïve in its suggestion that successful experiments with policy or technological innovation alone can drive politics. Indeed, politics is the heart of the problem, and no place has made this clearer in recent years than Latin America.

THE PINK TIDE, the wave of leftist governments that swept the region in the 2000s, both inherited and intensified a model of accumulation based on the extraction and export of natural resources. This model enabled important forms of socioeconomic inclusion and political empowerment for the masses, while simultaneously undermining more radical transformations including efforts to slow the pace of extraction and reverse environmental devastation. Between 2007 and 2017 in Ecuador, for example, leftist president Rafael Correa presided over a state that dramatically increased social spending and enjoyed widespread political support among the poor. His discourse resonated with a long history of popular calls for the nationalization of natural resources—and the use of resource rents to address social needs. Yet in 2011, four years into Correa's administration, more than a hundred social movement organizations and leftist political parties gathered for the Meeting of Social Movements for Democracy and Life and penned a manifesto that condemned the "extractivist model" of development. Over the next six years, conflict between the state and movements escalated, hinging on the socio-environmental harms of oil and mining development. The politics of extraction thus pitted a leftist government against a leftist resistance.

Such conflicts carry important consequences for combatting global warming. Though countries such as Ecuador contribute little to global emissions from the burning of fossil fuels, the oil and mining extraction that dominates their economies contributes to deforestation in vital ecosystems such as the Amazon. Protecting and regenerating tropical forests, especially by enforcing the territorial rights of Indigenous peoples, is essential for mitigating emissions.

Ecuador shows that militant anti-extractive movements are on the frontlines of the climate crisis. Dismantling extractivism—and the deep inequalities of the global order that reinforces it—is part and parcel of achieving climate safety.

Popular movements in Ecuador had long rebuked prior governments for being antidemocratic and neoliberal, but the anti-extractivist critique was new. In May 2012, in an interview in the Chilean leftist magazine *Punto Final*, and during protracted political conflict with many of these same social movements, Correa charged that rejecting the extractive model was a "colossal error." "Where in *The Communist Manifesto* does it say no to mining?" he asked. "What socialist theory says no to mining?" The fact that Correa felt compelled to mount such a defense reflects how central grassroots activists have been in the contentious politics of oil and mining. In dynamic conflict with state and corporate elites, popular mobilization shaped the political and economic consequences of resource extraction. And the stakes of these conflicts were high. Constitutional authority, democratic sovereignty, and the possibility of a post-neoliberal state hung in the balance. In this context, to think of solutions to the climate crisis and ecological devastation without a wholly new kind of radical politics would be impossible.

Indeed, just as the achievements of the left-in-power were limited by the contradictions of a particular political economic model, so the left-in-resistance came up against the contradictions of a critique and strategy centered on mobilizing those directly affected against extractive development. Anti-extractive movements can claim impressive accomplishments: they stalled specific extractive projects and reshaped the broader debate over resource extraction, forcing state actors and firms to respond to a new set of grievances and demands. But directly affected communities and allied environmental activists had difficulty assembling a popular sector coalition at the national scale with the power to articulate and enact an alternative to the extractive model. As a result, anti-extractivism has not yet succeeded in building a mass movement to match the scale and strength of the anti-neoliberal popular sector coalition that swept the leftist governments into office in the first place.

THIS EXAMPLE ILLUSTRATES how deeply politics matters. These two forms of leftism confronted one another in a dispute that became so polarized that each saw in the other a political enemy more dangerous than neoliberalism. Lost in this internecine dispute was the radical promise of twenty-first-century ecosocialism: collective, democratic control over the conditions of socio-natural existence.

Such a program could have coherently demanded both the redistribution of oil and mining revenues and a transition away from the extractive model of accumulation that generates those revenues. In fact, just such a vision inflected the 1994 political program of the Confederation of Indigenous Nationalities of Ecuador, published amidst massive mobilizations against neoliberal land reforms, that called for a "planned ecological communitarian economy." Yet two decades later, "socialism" and "anti-extractivism" had come to name two counterposed political projects. Socialism in Correa's usage meant state investment and spending in the pursuit of national development without transforming the model of accumulation or the class relations that it generates. Anti-extractivism referred to the militant defense of communities and ecosystems against the threat of oil extraction and mining without mobilizing the majority not immediately affected by social and environmental destruction.

The history of Ecuador also demonstrates how deeply the entire world economic order is implicated in the reproduction of extractivism, consigning the Global South to the losing end of economic—and ecological—exchange. As the global climate justice movement has long emphasized, confronting the climate crisis means transforming neocolonial relations. The places and peoples least responsible for the climate emergency are bearing the brunt of its deadly consequences.

Consider just one example. Activists pressured the Correa administration to adopt a civil society proposal to not extract oil from the Yasuní National Park, a UNESCO Biosphere Reserve and home to numerous Indigenous communities (some living in voluntary isolation), in exchange for $3.6 billion in donations from the international community to fund sustainable development (framed as the "ecological debt" owed by the Global North to the Global South). When the government failed to attract enough donations by the deadline, Correa decided to proceed with oil extraction, sparking the formation of the activist network YASunídos in 2013. Though the campaign did not achieve its goals, it drew huge protests in major cities far from the sites of extraction, and its size and reach rivaled the large protests against neoliberalism in the mid-2000s.

It is noteworthy that the YASunídos campaign directly contested Correa's claims that exploiting the Yasuní is necessary to fight poverty. By broadening the territorial base of anti-extractive protest and incorporating the historic economic concerns of other popular sectors, the campaign expanded the repertoire of anti-extractive resistance and drew connections across scales, from local ecosystem and communities to national policy and the international order itself. More recently, Latin American movements and left intellectuals have proposed a new "Ecosocial Pact" to transition the region to an economic model centered on socio-ecological flourishing—and have called for the cancellation of Latin America's unsustainable debt levels.

AS I WRITE, Latin America is teetering on the precipice between danger and hope. From Argentina's Mauricio Macri to Brazil's Jair Bolsonaro, reactionary governments have slashed social spending and eliminated environmental, social, and labor protections. Even when the right is voted out—as happened with Macri last year—its legacies generate enduring effects. Investor-friendly reforms in the oil and mining sectors are already expanding extraction, devastating ecosystems, and displacing Indigenous populations. Meanwhile, states reliant on exporting to global markets for their revenues find themselves with vanishingly little room for fiscal maneuver during the COVID-19 pandemic, depriving them of the resources needed to support their populations. But the scene is not entirely grim. The region has seen an efflorescence of social uprisings, with massive and successful demonstrations in the fall of 2019 in Ecuador and Chile, and, in October 2020, two decisive victories: for the left in Bolivia's elections, and for popular democracy in Chile's resounding vote in favor of rewriting the constitution that is a legacy of Augusto Pinochet's dictatorship.

At this moment of profound political uncertainty, it is worth highlighting the urgent necessity of both the left-in-power and the left-in-resistance. For the foreseeable future, achieving socioeconomic equality on a livable planet is the key political task for progressive movements everywhere. For all the limitations and contradictions of the Pink Tide, political, social, and economic inequalities will continue to reinforce one another without a left-in-power, denying a dignified life to the vast majority of the population and protecting the privileges of the few against the democratic will of the many. By the same token, for all of the challenges of building an anti-extractive mass movement, resistance against oil, coal, natural gas, and large-scale mining projects is absolutely vital if we are to avert the worst of climate chaos.

Despite the potential for conflict between them, these two projects are fundamentally intertwined. Global warming deepens inequality within and between countries, undermining a core goal of leftist governments. And wresting political power from fossil capital and democratizing state institutions is a prerequisite for meaningful action on climate change and other forms of environmental devastation. In other words, we need a new politics—not just new technologies and policies—to fight climate change and for a more just future.

PRIORITIZE VULNERABLE COMMUNITIES
Catherine Coleman Flowers

LIVING IN ALABAMA, a state bordered by the Gulf Coast, it is hard not to reflect on climate change and the environmental justice calamities that have been at the forefront of 2020. The pandemic has brought death to every corner of the world—and, as anticipated, vulnerable and marginalized communities have faced the highest death and infection rates. Next came the wildfires. So much of the world and the United States have been burning that adequate description conjures apocalyptic visions. Now we are in the midst of a historic hurricane season, battering the Gulf Coast over and again. There have been so many named storms this year that the twenty-five alphabetical names have been used up and we're now on to using Greek letters to designate them. As I write, we anxiously await the arrival of Zeta.

This year Mother Nature has previewed the destruction that is to come if climate change worsens and we continue to act as if humans are not its cause. Denial of climate change is not dissimilar to the denialism that causes so many to refuse to wear a mask and social distance to contain the spread of COVID-19. Denial doesn't prevent bad things from happening, and ignoring reality has caused traumatic consequences around the world. Lack of action will cause all of us to have the blood of future generations on our hands. And people are suffering now.

People living in communities plagued by environmental and climate injustice are already experiencing the effects of climate change—on the heels, for many, of having been traumatized by industrial pollution that has sickened them with cancers and other illnesses. Many in these communities are already doing what Charles Sabel and David G. Victor advise and are pursuing local climate activism and action. At the same time, many are also running up against the limits of what it is possible to achieve locally when global actions by states and moneyed corporations are stacked against them.

In Lowndes County, Alabama, climate change and a lack of adequate sanitation have intersected catastrophically. This county between Selma and Montgomery has a long history of racial terror, but its residents emerged as leaders during the civil rights era, helping to catalyze a political movement while the odds were against them. Today people in the county have emerged as activists against the neglect of rural communities while seeking environmental justice and climate justice. A few years ago, a peer-reviewed study found evidence of hookworm—a tropical parasite usually associated with the developing world—in fecal samples submitted by residents after a number of people were sickened mysteriously. Failed or no waste-water infrastructure was the culprit. The wastewater technology that is mandated by the state does not take into account the effects of climate change, such as rising water tables, extreme weather events, and increased rain. These climate change effects exacerbate inequalities already present as a result of poverty and state neglect, including the antiquated infrastructure, inadequate housing, and health disparities. The most vulnerable will suffer first, but no one is immune to the consequences of inaction.

In Florida, known for its many warm days and beautiful beaches, sea-level rise is already evident. As in Lowndes County, the groundwater is rising too. In Miami-Dade County, $3 billion worth of septic tanks infrastructure is failing, according to the *Miami Herald*. The leaky tanks are complicit in contaminating the aquifers which provide drinking water. Sea-level rise is also causing wealthier residents to move to higher ground, displacing people of color who are longtime residents of places such as Overtown, Little Haiti, and Elizabeth City. Segregated policies reinforced by redlining relegated people of color to these communities. Now climate gentrification is controlling where they can live once again.

In Alaska, water and sewer lines are being exposed and twisted because of thawing permafrost. Many Indigenous communities have never received water or wastewater infrastructure. The village of Newtok, for example, has no running water. With no toilets, people rely on five-gallon buckets to deal with their waste, which then goes into a pit or hole. Now the town is being relocated because increasing temperatures are causing the ground to melt out from under its homes.

In the Navajo Nation reservation that spans Arizona, New Mexico, Colorado, and Utah, many homes are likewise without running water or wastewater infrastructure. High rates of COVID-19 infection have underscored how difficult this makes it for residents to ensure something as simple as adequate handwashing.

In all of these stories, the people least responsible for climate change are the most impacted. It is the poor and marginalized who are, globally, most likely to be found in flood-prone areas, in heat islands, and in areas prone to wildfires, sea-level rise, pollution, and extreme weather.

In 2015, at the Twenty-First Conference of the Parties where the Paris Agreement was negotiated, the question was raised of how to help those for whom disaster brought about by climate change is not something that is coming but something that is already here. Although fortunately the 196 representatives agreed upon a plan to reduce climate change, this remains an open question not fully addressed by the agreement. Clearly, reductions in emissions are necessary to prevent *further* damage to communities already suffering in the United States, but that's not enough.

In a hopeful sign, the Biden-Sanders Unity Task Force on Climate Change acknowledged the unequal damage done by climate change: "The impacts of climate change are not evenly distributed in our society or our economy. Communities of color, low-income families, and indigenous communities have long suffered disproportionate and cumulative harm from air pollution, water pollution, and toxic sites." This statement is an excellent first step. To begin mitigating the injury, the United States should prioritize exposed, fence-line, frontline, and vulnerable communities. To rectify the harm, we must invest in making those communities more resilient to the impacts of climate crisis while providing for the documentation and remediation

of health impacts, all while rejoining the Paris Agreement and rati-
fying the Kigali Amendment to the Montreal Protocol. Americans
can lead the way in ensuring climate and environment justice now
and for generations to come.

Flowers

WHY THE PARIS AGREEMENT MATTERS
David Wallace-Wells

ON SEPTEMBER 22, Xi Jingping stepped before the UN General Assembly—virtually, of course—and offered a surprise announcement: China would aim to reach a peak in carbon emissions by 2030 and to reach carbon neutrality by 2060. This was a dramatic acceleration of Chinese ambition on decarbonization, one which single-handedly appeared to transform the global outlook, bringing the global goal established by the Paris Agreement—to keep warming below 2 degrees Celsius above the preindustrial average—back from the brink of impossibility.

Under what regime of global climate governance was this commitment made, and to what approach to climate geopolitics should it be credited? Under what regime or approach are its promises most likely to be realized, rather than discarded, as has nearly every emissions pledge ever made by any country in the entire history of pledged decarbonization?

I ask these questions—one backward looking, one forward looking—not because the answers are obvious but because they are murky, at best. The world is now five years past the negotiation of the Paris accords and four years past their signing, with, according to Climate Action Tracker, only Morocco and Gambia decarbonizing at a pace compatible with the goal of those accords. In this sense, with emissions and warming continuing essentially unchecked, the planet has left Paris behind. But no successor regime has yet replaced Paris, and the ad hoc climate geopolitics of recent years—Emmanuel Macron threatening to spike the Mercosur trade deal over Jair Bolsonaro's Amazon policies; the EU pledging a quarter of its COVID-19 stimulus to climate investments; Xi, a few weeks after his decarbonization pledge, calling the United States a "troublemaker" and "consensus-breaker" which had "seriously undermined global climate governance and cooperation"—still reflect the basic values of that agreement.

Charles Sabel and David G. Victor argue that a new model is needed, that the loose Paris regime has already proven inadequate to fulfill its own goals—indeed the goal of addressing the growth of carbon emissions at all. They suggest Paris is incapable not just of producing new commitments on the scale issued by Xi, but also of seeing the fulfillment of even much less significant existing commitments made by other countries. In other words, Paris can't be the answer to either of the critical questions above. "With so many diverse interests across so many countries," they write, "it has been hard to get global agreement simply on the need for action; *meaningful* consensus has been even more elusive."

I've had my doubts about Paris, too—beginning with the inadequacy of initial pledges, the loneliness of Morocco and Gambia in meeting them, and the seeming unlikelihood that countries would respond to those dispiriting early returns by accelerating their commitments rather than simply walking away from them. That the UN framework meant all nations could wield effective veto power over future agreements didn't seem to bode well, either, given how hard it was to imagine global climate unanimity. But Sabel and Victor's essay demonstrates the problem of trying to bury a global agreement too quickly. Presumably, that announcement from Beijing surprised them, too.

It's not just Beijing. When Donald Trump was elected president of the United States, vowing to withdraw from Paris, many analysts predicted it would be a devastating blow—another obituary written too quickly. While the Paris Agreement itself surely is not the only, or even primary, driver of accelerating ambition—others include extreme weather, climate activism, cultural changes amid growing public concern, the dramatic price decline of renewable energy, and the dramatic rise in the forecasted costs of warming impacts—it has been undeniably in the post-Paris era that global agreement on the need for action has been most firmly established, and in that period that meaningful consensus about its urgency has followed. Even in the midst of a global pandemic, under conditions that might have worried previous microgenerations of climate advocates, net-zero commitments have been made in 2020 not just by China but by the EU, Japan, and South Korea, each of them aiming to get there by 2050. Joe Biden's climate plan for the United States also calls for net zero by 2050. That makes almost three-quarters of the global economy, and more than 60 percent of current carbon emissions.

Pledges are just pledges, of course, and history counsels skepticism. Sabel and Victor suggest that an "experimentalist" approach to the problem is likely to prove more effective than a top-down approach. But, post-Paris, we are already "experimenting" with both national commitments and the policies that might make them real. Indeed, open-ended experimentalism is so much a part of the Paris approach that it has often been cited as its fatal flaw: emissions commitments and decarbonization targets are entirely voluntary, with neither enforcement nor encouragement mechanisms; goals are produced nation by nation, independent of the global 2-degree goal (this meant, at least at first, that the sum of national goals was totally insufficient to meet the global goal); the pathways to those national goals are left to the countries themselves, each contemplating a different mix of emissions and therefore a different mix of decarbonization strategies; pledges can be altered at any time (toward more ambition, it was hoped, but of course pledge-breaking was possible, too).

Over the last few years, the record of that experimentation was encouraging, if not yet sufficient to avoid dramatic warming. While the world is, to this point, falling far short of the Paris targets, it is also already doing much better than was feared just a few years ago. Coal, which grew terrifyingly fast during the first decade of the twenty-first century, is suddenly facing a much bleaker future. Renewables are already cheaper in most places—and poised to get so much cheaper that by decade's end they will cost less than even the "bridge fuel" of natural gas. Every year, the energy and emissions projections from even cautious institutions such as the International Energy Agency are revised downward, and the high-emissions scenario that was referred to until just a year or two ago as "business as usual" now appears, to most analysts, an impossible, beyond-worst-case projection.

Will it hold? For as long as climate has been discussed in the realm of geopolitics, the conversation has been complicated by the perception that decarbonization represents a collective action problem and the question of what enforcement or enticement mechanisms could "solve" it: since the benefits of decarbonization are distributed globally while costs are concentrated locally, some external force or structure was required, it was imagined, to bring the nations of the world into line. There was hope, for a time, that the UN could do that work, though, increasingly, analysts have echoed Sabel and Victor's skepticism about that. Over the last year, for instance, Yale economist William Nordhaus has called for the creation of a "climate club," built on the World Trade Organization model, which could recruit nations to the cause through the power of free trade. Similarly, historian Adam Tooze has argued that managing the green transition of developing economies will require the creation of a G40. Personally, I've cited the model of the nuclear nonproliferation agreements reached between the Soviet Union and the United States at the end of the Cold War as a model for possible bilateral dealmaking between today's two carbon superpowers, China and the United States. (In truth, that cooperation, which has grown more difficult, was a necessary precondition of the Paris accord, and would probably be required of any large-scale future agreement, as well.)

But as political scientists Matto Mildenberger and Michaël Aklin have recently found, it has not been primarily the collective action problem that has stymied global action but more local battles between the winners and losers of climate policy. (These are battles between uneven sides, to be sure, though the power of entrenched fossil fuel interests has been rapidly diminishing in the post-Paris world, along with their public valuations.) And the recent progress of our carbon trajectory away from worst-case and "business as usual" scenarios—progress almost improvised in the absence of any kind of new, post-Paris geopolitical regime—suggests at least the possibility that global governance may not be the determinative driver of progress or failure.

Instead, it now appears plausible that, at least in the short term, significant if insufficient decarbonization gains might be achieved all around the world without a successor regime to Paris—pledges and programs arising nation by nation, enacted largely according to the logic of national self-interest and cultural change. Depending on your perspective, this may sound naive (that the countries of the world might feel simply compelled to act, rather than policed into action) or cynical (that market logic will do more to bend curves than international agreements might). And whatever your perspective, such an ad hoc arrangement will prove inadequate, given that years of slow progress have effectively taken "safe" warming off the table.

It is also just the start. Later decarbonization will be more difficult, and the geopolitical challenges arising from new energy regimes are not yet so clearly in view, as Jason Bordoff, director of the Center on Global Energy Policy, has recently written. It may yet prove critical to "police" the bad behavior of recalcitrant nations through enticements, sanctions, and more. But for now, this recent

Wallace-Wells

progress is far more encouraging than what came before the Paris accords. It also happens to be precisely the future that Christiana Figueres, the former head of the UN Framework Convention on Climate Change who presided over Paris, has been predicting in the wake of the agreement's "failure." Our climate timeline doesn't allow for much more failure, even the partial kind. But let's maybe not toss Paris into the trash bin just yet.

POLITICS IS PLASTIC
Charles Sabel & David G. Victor

THESE THOUGHTFUL RESPONSES make two main charges. First, we fail to give priority to the raw politics of redistribution posed by climate change. Second, we imagine that technical problem-solving happens independently of a clash of interests—or perhaps even substitutes for political struggle.

We plead guilty to the first charge, but for a reason that, at least so far as our intentions are concerned, absolves us from the second. We don't put politics first for the same reason that we don't put policy or problem-solving first: in a social transition as profound and uncertain as decarbonization, the two are inseparable. Citizens, firms, interest groups, and political parties can't define their interests without some view of what's actually feasible—and what potential allies regard as feasible, too—even as new possibilities emerge from these provisional commitments.

In these times especially, both politics and interests are plastic. Experimentalism seeks to make this fact both politically visible and politically productive. It entails putting developments under the direction of penalty defaults based on a thin consensus about goals. It means pressuring potential veto players to change strategy and coalition partners. It involves correcting central decisions in light of local mobilization and experience, but also challenging decisions in any locale in view of developments in other similar places and encouraging mutual correction of expert and lay knowledge. Understood this way, the experimentalist approach meshes well—perhaps even helps further define—Robert C. Hockett's vision of the Green New Deal, which, as he sees it, crucially depends on organized consultation between national centers and local communities.

Jessica Green advances the politics-first thesis most directly. "Until governments address the conflicts between the winners and losers of climate change and climate policy," she writes, "experimentalist governance will be limited in its ambition and impact." In a similar vein, Alyssa Battistoni states that "challenging the power of the fossil fuel industry is the sine qua non of climate politics." Thea Riofrancos makes a cognate claim in her canvass of Latin America: pointing to the conflicts between Pink Tide national governments and local, anti-extractivist movements, she asserts that "politics is the heart of the problem." And Catherine Coleman Flowers reminds us that although many local communities are "pursuing local climate activism . . . many are also running up against the limits of what it is possible to achieve locally when global actions by states and moneyed corporations are stacked against them." Power and politics set the limits once again.

We do not mean to minimize the importance of distributional fights or politics generally: they have an essential and in any case inevitable role to play. Still less do we mean to convey the economy will simply decarbonize itself, without active institutional development and regulatory oversight: there is painstaking work to be done. Where we disagree is with the claim that political questions have to be resolved *in advance* before problem-solving can begin. Our grounds are not just theoretical but empirical. Just as the effort to solve the free-rider problem has paralyzed global climate change efforts, an ex ante focus on getting the politics right could inadvertently stall domestic action.

In Green's conception, power is rooted in the ownership of assets such as factories and houses. Some destroy the climate; others are vulnerable to its destruction. The paramount political problem for climate change, as Green sees it, is preventing owners of the former type from blocking reforms that devalue their property and ultimately threaten their way of life. This veto power can be checked, Green argues, by sufficiently detailed legislation—it takes more than the "thin consensus" of experimentalism. If legislation proves too ambiguous, veto power can be limited by regulation, provided the regulator has already resolved the "fundamental conflicts of existential politics before" engaging in experimentalist problem-solving—as was the case, Green maintains, with CARB. If regulation fails, nationalization is a possibility, and so on.

We—like the overwhelming majority of Americans—have no doubt that politics can have existential stakes. Nor do we doubt that some actors tied to climate-destroying interests see any other activity as a kind of social death. Green's other claims, though, are dubious. Asset types are not set in stone; a factory that destroys the climate now need not destroy it forever. The interplay of technical innovation and constraints from politics and regulation opens new possibilities. Until a decade ago, the car industry was mostly against decarbonization. Now, many companies—not all, but enough—are competing to produce electric cars, and a great deal of new investment is aimed there. Politics—but not exclusively politics—helped to make that happen, in part with regulatory measures that encouraged new directions in technological innovation and helped shape consumer behavior. Shifts in investment have, in turn, shifted political power.

Or consider veto-stopping remedies. Green's contention that CARB had definitively resolved conflicts with car companies before engaging in problem-solving ignores decades of often contentious exchange between manufactures and regulators, when standards were proposed and revised as judgments of feasibility shifted. We doubt that the outcome—starting with the question of whether such collaboration would work—was in any sense a foregone conclusion to the participants. In any case, how can we tell when the power question is truly "settled"? Some will say: when the state expropriates the assets of the fossil fuel industries. But it is far from clear that we should place such high confidence in nationalization as a remedy. Observers often point to Equinor as a model of the "greening" of a state-owned oil company. But its success depends in large part on the culture of hyper-green Norway, on being well managed, and on its alliance with other firms—few of which are state-owned. Across most of the rest of the oil industry, state ownership is hardly synonymous with innovation or transformation. It is hard—sometimes impossible—to identify in advance a remedy that works for good.

Leah C. Stokes's recent account of state-level fights over renewable portfolio standards—which dictate the stepwise introduction of renewable energy sources to a state's power grid—cuts the same way. Stokes's central argument is that the political struggle over such standards typically continues after initial legislation, after regulatory rule-making, and indeed after any point that one side or the other might have thought settled the question once and for all. The principal reason is what Stokes calls the "fog of enactment"—uncertainty about how a decision will work out in practice that makes surprises likely. Unpleasant surprises trigger reconsideration and maneuvering for do-overs. The contest only stops (for a time) when environmentalists' successes become self-reinforcing or fossil fuel interests erect barriers to that outcome. But even in cases such as Arizona, where Stokes reports that opponents strongly influence electoral politics and regulatory decisions, dramatic reversals are still possible. As we write in early November, Arizona regulators voted just days ago to require 100 percent clean electricity on the grid by 2050: incumbent utilities, after a number of pyrrhic political victories, and seeing ways forward in the experience of neighboring states, have come to accept the inevitability of decarbonization. Interests and politics shift as facts change and as key players learn what's at stake.

Riofrancos's case study only further reveals the limits of the ex ante redistributivist approach. The leftist governments that swept power in Brazil, Argentina, Ecuador, and Bolivia in the 2000s promised to redistribute the proceeds of the commodity boom to disadvantaged groups—though not the ones whose ways of life were harmed most directly by the boom itself. When those groups raised redistibutivist demands of their own, the result was the intractable conflict Riofrancos describes. The same focus on fixed but incompatible ideas of justice that made it all but impossible for compromise impeded rather than facilitated progress. When the boom passed, they were left where they had started, and economic disappointment was compounded—especially among many supporters of Pink Tide governments—by a sense of political betrayal.

Seeing politics as plastic helps to explain the good news, shared by David Wallace-Wells, that many places *are* acting on climate—from the European Green Deal to recent plans to achieve net-zero emissions in China (by 2060) and Korea (by 2050). The groundwork in all these cases follows our logic of experimentalism. No party has focused on resolving the distributional political conflicts first. It helps that each thinks, as well, that it is building the industries of the future and that some of those firms, now able to attract more investment, are getting more powerful. Paris may play a modest role in continuing to focus political attention, but the most important drivers are the shifting politics made possible by real investments and experimentation. The reality is that centralized, consensus-oriented decision-making isn't going to drive a revolution.

Hockett's vision of the Green New Deal—however it must be rescaled in light of election results—offers an alternative approach to decarbonization that converges in many ways with our own. The goals are not fixed at the outset; neither does reform start from a comprehensive and enduring political settlement. Goals, and the politics to support them, emerge from a series of legislative initiatives in a decade-long process. A key institutional innovation, however, is designed to make goal-setting more inclusive and politics more participatory and democratic: local committees are to be established across the land to ensure that frontline voices are heard. Hockett suggests that the first task of these committees will be to agree on the best use of additional resources allocated to them.

This may well be the best way to kick-start participation. But in our view, these committees will only succeed if their connection to the center is ongoing and reciprocal: ongoing, because local understanding of local problems will change both with the experience of trying to solve them and increased awareness of what works elsewhere; reciprocal, because—as Flowers and Riofrancos observe—there are many problems that local communities can only solve in collaboration with higher levels of government.

As Hockett makes clear in his new book, *Financing the Green New Deal*, these local links are only one part of a structure that aims to facilitate public–private collaboration; cooperation across federal, state, and local levels; and coordination among the many diverse policy areas that meet in decarbonization. But even in isolation from this larger structure, the lattice of local–center committees illustrates just the kind of "political innovation" Battistoni calls for: "figuring out how to deploy technologies we already have to cut carbon as quickly as possible, in ways that build constituencies for further climate action." Building these innovations—those that speed accountable deployment of the technologies we have and those that speed development of those we still need to invent—is itself a political task, recasting interests and institutions together. That is the task to which we must turn to save the climate.

ESSAYS

ESSAYS

POISONING TALLEVAST

James A. Manigault-Bryant, Ruby Bagwyn, &
José A. Constantine

TALLEVAST, FLORIDA, is a predominantly Black, unincorporated community between Manatee and Sarasota Counties. If anyone outside of the area knows of the town of fewer than eighty homes spread across two square miles, it is likely because, about twenty years ago, its groundwater was discovered to have been poisoned by the manufacture of weapons-grade beryllium during the Cold War.

The plot will sound familiar: a polluting industry, privately owned but authorized by the state, is placed near Black homes, fouls the natural resources, and causes irreversible harm to the community's health. Environmental racism is global, but it is particularly common to Black communities in the U.S. South, where state authorities tend to allow more latitude to industrial polluters. Consider Warren County, North Carolina, where a dump for the neurotoxin PCB was sited adjacent to the homes of poor Blacks. Or Louisiana's "Cancer Alley," where petrochemical production has devastated dozens of Black communities along the banks of the Mississippi. Such occurrences extend the timeframe of plantation-like mechanisms of control and dispossession. Of course, it's not only in the South. Change a couple key details and you have Flint, Michigan, or Secunda, South Africa.

In 1996 the defunct Loral American Beryllium Company (ABC) was purchased by Lockheed Martin, the world's largest defense contractor and the top employer of Florida's industrial workforce. The acquisition extended Lockheed's already notable presence in Florida, which has been continuous since 1956 when, as Martin Marietta, it established a missile plant in Orlando. Once it procured ABC, Lockheed worked with Florida governmental agencies to hide ABC's sins from Tallevast residents. The collusion is documented in over 1,800 documents held in Florida's public environmental records database. By combing through these records—which include memos, interoffice emails, meeting minutes, and environmental assessments—we have been able to reconstruct the story of how, between 2000 and 2004, corporate and state actors knowingly withheld information from Tallevast residents about the contamination in their community.

A BARREN PATCH OF LAND on Tallevast's main road still marks where the ABC plant stood. Across the street is the Sarasota Bradenton International Airport (SRQ), which increasingly welcomes sports stars traveling to IMG Academy, recent host of the WNBA's COVID bubble. On the other side of SRQ lie the Ringling Museum of Art and New College of Florida, the state's prestigious liberal arts institution. At Tallevast's boundaries are an office park for the pretzel maker Snyder's of Hanover and Suncoast Golf Center, a three par golf course, where on any given day elderly white men practice their midrange strokes.

Before Sarasota's postindustrial commercial sprawl began squeezing the life from it, Tallevast possessed a vitality of southern Blackness. On Fridays and Saturdays, the smell of barbequed meat from grills on front lawns wafted through the air and the energy of youth reverberated in the streets—competitive pickup basketball games on outdoor courts, motorized bikes roaring on pavement. And on Sundays, Baptist, Methodist, and Holiness churches gathered to worship and remember how far they had come. After praise services, at least in earlier generations, residents would reconvene for picnics on the turquoise waters of Sarasota Bay, just over a mile away.

Mrs. Helen Heathington spoke of Tallevast's golden days at a January 2019 community meeting. Then ninety-three, making her the oldest living member of the community, she was part of the third generation of Tallevast residents, a grandchild of one of the founding families who had migrated to the small town when it was a labor camp for the Tallevast family's turpentine business. Educated in Manatee County schools, Heathington then earned a degree in nursing from Florida Agricultural and Mechanical University (FAMU) before entering the United States Air Force. After being stationed all over the world, she returned to Tallevast in the 1970s with her husband, Clifford, to raise their three children, so that the community could help instill in them the values it had given her. "It was a place you could raise your children without too much worry," she would often tell young people during community meetings, "because you knew there was always someone watching them. . . . Most of the people

. . . all worked hard to keep their children in school and send them off to college for a better life."

In the early days, residents of Tallevast were subject both to Jim Crow racism and geographic discrimination. Heathington told of how Manatee County would not even provide Tallevast's students with transportation to the county's one segregated Black high school. Instead, Mr. Ulysses "Rip" Ward, who operated a group of day laborers, would drive the students to school in Palmetto, thirty minutes away. The vehicle, an "old bread truck" with benches nailed in the back, would break down periodically and make the students late for school. If the students arrived late for morning assembly, the principal would stop mid-sentence and say, "And here comes Tallevast!" Tallevast children were not only humiliated by their inferior mode of school transportation, but also by how their principal repeatedly brought attention to it in a way that reinforced beliefs about the rural community's lack of decorum and intelligence.

Despite general neglect—Tallevast was one of the last towns in Manatee County to receive street lights, paved roads, telephone lines, and sidewalks—for at least two generations the community's young people went to college at a higher rate than students in other Manatee County districts. Heathington and her sister Mrs. Lillian Granderson were among Tallevast's first residents to finish a four-year degree. After them, Tallevast would send four or five young people to college each year. As in many Black communities, education was seen as a salvation, a catalyst for the community's growth. Elders hoped their children would acquire knowledge and bring it back to Tallevast for its continued evolution.

When Visioneering, a small industrial plant for engineering metals, was built in the center of Tallevast in 1957, residents hoped it would bring jobs and development. Four years later, Visioneering's machining became focused on beryllium, and the company changed its name to American Beryllium Company (ABC). Beryllium is a metal used for missiles, rockets, and nuclear reactors because of its lightness, strength, and capacities to conduct electricity at high temperatures. Because the machining of beryllium generates toxic dust and requires organic solvents for cleaning, a system was installed to mitigate the dangers, including subsurface sumps to collect wastewater and a 9,000-square-foot artificial evaporation pond to hold effluent.

While all ABC workers were likely exposed to beryllium levels that exceeded legal limits, its custodial workers, some of whom were Tallevast residents, were more likely than others to contract berylliosis (chronic pulmonary granulomatosis), a chronic and incurable disease that scars lung tissue, shortening the breath and stressing the heart. One resident, Mr. Charles Ziegler, contracted berylliosis from working as a janitor at ABC for over twenty years. Before ABC, he was an independent roofer, but switched to ABC because it paid much better, providing him a wage of between $15 and $17 an hour. As an ABC custodian, Ziegler vacuumed beryllium dust from the tables holding machining equipment, filtered the dust into bags, and transported the bags to bathhouses where he dumped the dust into a drum. After capping the drums, he washed the bags and then shipped them off site for recycling or further disposal. "I liked the work at American Beryllium," he told a focus group of former ABC employees in 2012. "The work wasn't hard, not hard at all.

They didn't push you too hard. . . . [But I] didn't know anything about beryllium—[it was] no different [to me] than a grain of sand."

Ziegler had little control over the "charcoal-like" beryllium dust. It would seep out from the bags and spill from capped drums. "It didn't make any difference how you did it," he explained to his colleagues during the 2012 focus group, "the dust would escape because it was so light." Other employees would wash the bathhouses that contained the drums of beryllium, which would then disperse the dust into the community. Ziegler held a clear memory of this: "Do you know where all that stuff went to? On the road, see? . . . They'll never get rid of all of it. And I guarantee . . . if you would . . . tear it down, you could go over there, and I bet you'll find some beryllium." Ziegler lived across the street from the facility and would bring the dust home with him: "Yeah, you take it home. Take it home in my clothes." Ziegler's wife, Beatrice, and her brother, Leroy Mazon, who lived with them, also developed berylliosis.

Despite the risks of beryllium machining, Manatee County officials reported in 1992 that ABC was not considered an "environmentally regulated site." But the Florida Department of Environmental Protection (FDEP) consistently monitored ABC, conducting at least seven inspections between 1982 and 1995. And even with knowledge of the dangers of beryllium dust, FDEP did not monitor its aerial dispersal as strongly because ABC drummed and shipped it for recycling to Brush-Wellman, Inc., the country's largest beryllium supplier, in Ohio.

Nonetheless, the dangers of beryllium dust had been documented since at least the 1940s, and even more specifically at the ABC facility in the mid-1980s by Dr. Lee Newman, then head of the Division of Environmental and Occupational Health Services at National Jewish Medical and Research Center. Newman found that there were no barriers between the machinery and the front office at ABC, and its lathes and grinding machines were not confined to individual rooms as at other plants, increasing laborers' risk of exposure to beryllium dust.

Of greater concern to FDEP in its multiple inspections was the forty types of organic solvents used to degrease products and mill instruments during the daily operations. This liquid waste was funneled through floor drains and into sumps, each up to 105 cubic feet in size, about the size of a compact car. For years, FDEP inspections vouched that solvent waste was being drummed and shipped to off-site chemical waste facilities. But in fact, much of the waste was simply remaining in on-site storage tanks.

In 1996 Lockheed Martin acquired ABC when it purchased the Loral Corporation. The following year, Lockheed hired Tetra Tech, an environmental consulting firm, to conduct environmental and facility assessments to prepare the property for sale. Tetra Tech initially found that the site was in compliance with all state environmental regulations. After cleanup target levels for soil and groundwater contamination changed in 1999, however, Tetra Tech was forced to revise its reporting. On January 20, 2000, Tetra Tech and Lockheed disclosed to the Manatee County Environmental Action Commission that petroleum levels in soil exceeded the new standards. In a separate letter sent to the same agency eight days later, they then disclosed that groundwater had been contaminated with organic solvents and metals from "an unidentified source."

The facility assessment report that Tetra Tech had conducted in 1997, which initially held ABC in compliance with target levels, actually revealed that sumps contained solvents and that on-site storage containers were full of solvent waste. Lockheed Martin reported the contamination in 2000, but it is unclear when the company first realized that waste storage containers were leaking solvent- and metal-tarnished wastewater into the soil and groundwater. During these interagency exchanges about the deadly toxins flowing beneath Tallevast, no one in the community was notified.

Of all the solvents that ended up poisoning the groundwater, the one that caused the most concern was trichloroethylene (TCE). For much of the twentieth century, TCE was common in dry cleaning, as an anesthetic, and as an industrial cleaner. The pervasiveness of TCE meant that exposure to the chemical was widespread. The health impacts of TCE exposure have been known since at least 1915, but epidemiological studies conducted in the 1950s revealed that sustained exposure to TCE is linked to a variety of psychological disorders and significantly higher risks of kidney cancer, liver cancer, Hodgkin's and non-Hodgkin's lymphoma, cervical cancer, and prostate cancer. In 1977 the federal government listed TCE as a priority pollutant in the Clean Water Act; in 1982, the Environmental Protection Agency (EPA) identified TCE as a serious threat to drinking water, establishing a maximum allowable concentration of 5 micrograms per liter (ug/L) of drinking water.

Tetra Tech published a Contamination Assessment Report for ABC in April 2001. Organic solvents were found in thirteen monitoring wells on the ABC site. The highest reported level of

TCE was 1,500 ug/L—300 times the EPA's maximum contaminant level. Tetra Tech concluded that organic solvents "may be migrating off-site" and created an illustration that displayed the known extent of organic solvents exceeding groundwater cleanup criteria. Question marks traced the northern and eastern borders of the property, each one signifying that contaminants may have dispersed into the community.

Nearly a year later, on March 5, 2002, Lockheed Martin and Tetra Tech informed the FDEP of what had been discovered the previous year. Organic solvents "are migrating off-site," the report states, and further investigation would be needed to determine the extent of contamination. In its "Interim Data Report and Contamination Assessment Plan Addendum #2," published on September 13, 2002, Tetra Tech provided analytical results from the sampling of twenty-three on- and off-site wells. TCE was detected at concentrations above the EPA's maximum contaminant level in fifteen of them. The highest reported level of TCE was 4,300 ug/L—860 times the federal standard.

In Tetra Tech's "Final Contamination Assessment Report" released in May 2003, a figure illustrates a menacing plume of TCE beneath fourteen homes in Tallevast. But no one told residents that the water beneath them had been poisoned. Conservative estimates of hydraulic conductivity, or the speed that groundwater can be transmitted through soil, indicate that it would have taken four decades for the plume to achieve its size on the 2003 map. It appears that ABC was actively contaminating the groundwater from the start of its operations in 1962.

JUST AS SYSTEMIC RACISM delayed the arrival of basic amenities to Tallevast, residents were brought to municipal water unevenly. Shortly after ABC installed one of its first on-site monitoring wells in 1985 to detect potential contamination on its own premises, Manatee County received a Housing and Urban Development Community Block Development Grant of $1 million to install water and sewer lines in Tallevast. When the funds were exhausted, many community members still had no municipal water, which put them in direct contact with toxins leaking from ABC. The prevalence of wells was common knowledge in the community, but it took state and local agencies two years after Lockheed first divulged the contamination to FDEP to even consider identifying them.

At a March 5, 2002, meeting of representatives from FDEP, Lockheed Martin, and Tetra Tech, the assembled determined: "A private well search needs to be conducted. . . . [P]roperty owners and tenants may also need to be contacted via phone or letter. FDEP will contact the Department of Health regarding permitted wells in the surrounding area." But instead of contacting the Manatee County Department of Health, FDEP waste cleanup supervisor Michael Gonsalves sent FDEP environmental specialist Kimberly Brooks to Tallevast to look for wells on March 26, 2002. The following day, she emailed Gonsalves to report that she had been to Tallevast and spotted a number of wells, but that her search had been limited because she had at no point exited her car. She wrote that she found Tallevast "very unkempt (to put it mildly)." Brooks then sent a number of emails to

Andy Reich, environmental manager of the Florida Department of Health's Drinking Water Toxics Program, to ask for assistance. Reich in turn dispatched Tom Larkin of the Manatee County Department of Health to search for wells. In an email dated August 7, 2002, Reich shared an image of the area of suspected wells, offered his contacts to support the search, and expressed gratitude to Larkin for his assistance. It remains unknown what Larkin found.

In its May 2003 Final Contamination Assessment Report, Tetra Tech writes that "no private wells are being used . . . in the vicinity of the site." The FDEP did not dispute this assertion, despite knowing that Brooks's survey, cursory as it may have been, had identified multiple wells. Yet Tetra Tech's insistence that there were no private wells in Tallevast enabled them to claim, with the FDEP's endorsement, that residents were not exposed to contaminated groundwater, and so they did not need to be informed about the toxic plume beneath their homes.

The March 5, 2002, meeting also occasioned a debate about where to install monitoring wells for delineating the extent of the contamination. Tetra Tech indicated that these wells would "be completed within the public right-of-way or on private residences," but Gonsalves advised that it would be more efficient to install wells on public property. While the decision on where to place monitoring wells was internally framed as a "private" versus "public" matter, the conversation, much like Brooks's disparaging description of Tallevast, was racially coded. Tallevast's Black residents, and the homes in which they lived, were not deemed worth the effort to fulfill the agency's mission to protect the public.

IT WAS NOT UNTIL September 2003—over three years after Lockheed Martin informed county and state officials of the contamination—that community members became even loosely aware of what was transpiring in Tallevast. An oft-told story is that resident Mrs. Laura Ward, encountering a crew of men operating a drilling rig in her yard one afternoon, asked them what they were doing, to which they responded, "You don't know, but the water is contaminated here." Another resident, Mrs. Wanda Washington, is said to have learned of the contamination from a repairman who was denied a permit to work on a trailer behind one of the community's churches, Bryant Chapel, because of the trailer's suspected contamination. When Ward and Washington together approached local and regional agencies to ask what was going on, they got the runaround: a Manatee County Health Department official sent them to the FDEP Southwest District Office in Tampa; FDEP encouraged them to talk to Lockheed.

When they finally learned in early 2004 that the FDEP had been making enquiries about residential wells, Ward was immediately able to supply a list of twenty-five residences that utilized well water. After facing pressure from the community and local media, the FDEP agreed to test them to determine if they had been contaminated by solvents.

On May 20, 2004, the agencies sampled seventeen wells, but with media pressure mounting, Deborah Getzoff, director of the FDEP Southwest District Office, assured the public that "private drinking-water wells in Tallevast are not threatened by pollutants from the former American Beryllium site." She could not have been more wrong. TCE concentrations were above drinking water standards in five of the wells sampled that day, ranging from 7.4 ug/L to 220 ug/L—44 times the EPA's maximum contaminant level.

OFFICIALS FROM STATE and county agencies attributed their failure to mitigate contaminant exposure to a disintegration of interagency communication. Charles Henry, environmental health director of the Manatee County Health Department, wrote on May 15, 2004, that his department "first became aware of the health concerns of residents and the potential for off-site groundwater contamination near the former American Beryllium plant when the local media printed the first story on May 1, 2004"—four years after Lockheed Martin had notified the FDEP.

The Manatee County Environmental Protection Department also claimed not to have discovered the contamination until 2004. *Sarasota Herald-Tribune* reporter Scott Carroll published an article on May 15, 2004, in which he interviewed Karen Collins-Fleming, director of the Manatee County Environmental Protection Department. "Collins-Fleming said she never saw a letter Lockheed Martin sent the county in 2000 notifying it of the pollution and can't find it anywhere in the county's file," Carroll wrote. "The DEP only sent the county a couple of reports on the testing and cleanup efforts out of the dozen or so submitted." Collins-Fleming adamantly claimed that "this basically has been an issue between DEP and the owner. Since they don't have any requirement to pull us into the loop, we were unaware."

The professed collapse in interagency communication extended to the farcical searches for wells. When Paul Panik of the Manatee County Environmental Protection Department inspected the county utility billing records on May 10, 2004, he realized that at least thirteen residences were not paying to be connected to the public water supply. With just this cursory search, Panik had already identified four of the five residences whose wells were known to have concentrations of TCE above drinking water standards. If the FDEP had asked the county to examine its financial records earlier, it would have recognized that a number of other Tallevast residents were not connected to the public water supply.

In fact, the FDEP had to look no further than its own office for information about residential wells in Tallevast: it already held *three* reports from other projects that identified private wells in the community. But even if officials were unaware of the three reports of wells, or doubted the results of Kimberly Brooks's search, Lockheed Martin informed Gonsalves that it "had identified what they believed were potable wells near the [former American Beryllium] site to the east (1-2 blocks) of the railroad tracks" during the March 5, 2002, meeting. FDEP held in its own building information it spent months half-heartedly trying to track down outside of it. Meanwhile residents continued to drink water that contained trichloroethylene.

AS THE REALITIES of the contamination became clearer to the community, Heathington, drawing on her experience as a registered nurse, conducted a health survey of Tallevast residents in 2005. Visiting with every family in Tallevast, she found fifteen cases of cancer spread across the community's eighty-seven homes, as well as high rates of miscarriage, sterility, and neurological disorders. Heathington's discoveries convinced her of the need for a systematic study by state officials.

Three years later, the Agency for Toxic Substances and Disease Registry (ATSDR) and the Florida Department of Health's (FDOH) Division of Environmental Health ran statistical studies assessing the risk of residents getting ill from their exposure to the contaminants measured by the FDEP. Using data from two databases, the Florida Cancer Data System and the Florida Bureau of Vital Statistics, FDOH concluded that while there was a slightly higher number of expected cancers, "causality cannot be assessed" because of the small sample size of residents and the agency's professed inability to verify the addresses of community members. A test with interviews and surveys would yield more conclusive results, it advised, although no state agencies have provided any kind of study since the ATSDR conducted one in 2008.

F.O.C.U.S., a local advocacy group led by Tallevast residents Ward and Washington, commissioned the most detailed public health investigation of Tallevast residents so far. In the final two months of 2010, when environmental consultants measured beryllium dust around the ABC site at 250 times acceptable levels, a team of public health researchers led by Janvier Gasana, then an Associate Professor at Florida International University Robert Stempel College of Public Health and Social Work, surveyed almost 70 percent of Tallevast residents about their health, and acquired medical records of over 150 residents from other databases monitored by the state of Florida. Gasana's results illustrated the deterioration of residents' health. He confirmed that there were 78 cases of cancer diagnosed in current and former Tallevast residents from 1962 to 2010, concluding that "the overall cancer incidence among Tallevast residents was 85% higher than among the Florida African Americans." Gasana also determined that "cancers were positively associated with drinking well water among people who never used filtration and were born in Tallevast after 1962."

The Florida Department of Health challenged Gasana's methodology after reviewing his completed report in 2012. Although his methodology was approved by an independent expert and supported by state senator Bill Galvano, the FDOH refused to endorse it, effectively stalling, and at this point eliminating, any kind of state-mandated response to Gasana's clear delineation of a cancer cluster in Tallevast.

THE TALLEVAST COMMUNITY has sought restitution through Florida's courts and legislature. Since 2011 F.O.C.U.S. has filed a series of ultimately unsuccessful suits against FDEP challenging the agency's approval of Lockheed's remedial action plans. Residents have also filed lawsuits against Lockheed Martin. For instance, in 2007 Ziegler and his family sued Lockheed for their contraction of berylliosis; the case was settled in 2011 for an undisclosed amount. The largest suit, *Laura Ward v. Lockheed Martin Corporation*, included over 200 residents who sought monetary damages for the contamination of their properties, and for the distress caused by Lockheed's failure to inform them of what had transpired. Filed in 2005, the case was settled for an undisclosed amount in 2010. Many residents felt that the settlement did not come close to covering what they had lost in land, homes, and community.

Outside of the courts, the Tallevast case led legislators to change the FDEP's notification procedures for environmental contamination. A Committee Substitute for House Bill 937, also known as the "Tallevast Bill," now obligates FDEP to inform residents within thirty days of reported environmental contamination of their homes and properties. Sponsored by Senator Galvano, and signed into law by Governor Jeb Bush in 2005, the legislation might spare other communities from polluters withholding information about leaked waste, and from the incompetent responses of Florida agencies to toxic spills. Although the bill and the settlements concluded Tallevast's story in the press, neither remedy has, in any meaningful sense, saved Tallevast.

That Tallevast has not received satisfactory recompense from the state for the near destruction of its community is hardly surprising. National protests in recent months have brought public attention to state-coordinated assaults on Black lives through urban renewal, sterilization, and, of course, police brutality. In Tallevast, the state acted no less maliciously by ignoring and then concealing the community's poisoning by a private arm of the military–industrial complex. In failing to hold Lockheed and Loral Corporation accountable for poisoning Tallevast, Florida local and state authorities reinforced structural racism, and aligned themselves with U.S. ambitions to police the world. Legal and then de facto segregation created racial boundaries that separated Tallevast from equal education, civic amenities, and clean air and water; Cold War capitalist profiteering sickened Tallevast's residents and looted their property.

ADJACENT TO THE PLOT that was recently emptied of ABC's last remains is a new edifice that stands out from the older properties in Tallevast. Painted peach pastel and burnt orange, it resembles homes found in more exclusive sections of Sarasota and Manatee Counties. The pristine building, a state-of-the-art water treatment facility owned and operated by Lockheed Martin, is shrouded in secrecy. The facility processes groundwater pulled in from over seventy wells located throughout the community, removing contaminants and dumping treated water into surrounding wetlands. Lockheed Martin has to periodically apply for permission from the Manatee County Utilities Department to release the effluent, applications that will be a regular occurrence during the fifty to hundred years that it is expected to take for the groundwater to finally be cleaned.

The expensive remediation process is increasingly more for the benefit of the industrial development enclosing Tallevast than it is for the Tallevast community itself. This fall, the Manatee County Board of Commissioners approved the rezoning of former residential and agricultural properties for industrial use to make way for the construction of warehouses that will house offices for a Fortune 500 firm. When Tallevast residents contested the rezoning proposal out of concern for how new construction will affect the groundwater treatment, the board claimed it will rely on FDEP's oversight to ensure the community's safety.

While Manatee County reimagines the future of Tallevast's land, its community is undergoing a generational shift. Ziegler succumbed to berylliosis in 2017, convinced that Tallevast residents would have never allowed ABC inside the community if they had known what beryllium production could do to their bodies—what it ultimately did to his body. Last January, Heathington passed away, about a week after her ninety-fourth birthday. When she told the story of the old, unreliable bread truck that made her and her Tallevast classmates late for school, she would often end on a note of pride about the fact that Tallevast residents were property owners—something few Blacks in the county could say. "[T]hey would laugh at things about kids from Tallevast," she would divulge with a slight grin, "because we were from the country, not knowing that most of the people from Tallevast owned [the land] they had . . . and could do what they wanted with it." Owning land was meant to lead community members inexorably toward future prosperity. Now most of that land—poisoned by hostile forces that the founding families could not have imagined a century ago—remains in the hands of their descendants, who must determine what is to come.

CLIMATE CHANGE'S NEW ALLY, BIG FINANCE

Madison Condon

OVER THE PAST TWO YEARS, a striking change has taken place in the boardrooms of greenhouse-gas producers: a growing number of large companies have announced commitments to achieve net-zero emissions by 2050. These include the oil majors BP, Shell, and Total, the mining giant Rio Tinto, and the electricity supplier Southern Company. While such commitments are often described as "voluntary"—not mandated by government regulation—they were often adopted begrudgingly by executives and boards acquiescing to demands made by a coordinated group of their largest shareholders.

This group, Climate Action 100+, is an association of many of the world's largest institutional investors. With over 450 members, it manages a staggering $40 trillion in assets—roughly 46 percent of *global* GDP. Founded in 2017, the coalition initially was made up mostly of pension funds and European asset managers, but its ranks have grown rapidly, and last winter both J.P. Morgan and Black-Rock (the world's largest asset manager) became signatories to the association's pledge to pressure portfolio companies to reduce emissions and disclose financial risks related to climate change.

Some critics think corporate net-zero goals smack of greenwashing. That is a legitimate concern, but many of the latest commitments contain details that suggest they are more than just PR moves. Shareholders have pressed for tying executive compensation directly to the achievement of emissions goals. And some companies have begun to write down billions of dollars of fossil assets they previously claimed would be profitably sold. Emissions targets are not the only change investors are fighting for, either; they have been paying increasing attention to corporations' efforts to thwart carbon regulation. This summer, for example, Chevron's management lost a battle against a shareholder proposal demanding the company reveal how much money it spends lobbying and change its expenditures to align with the goals of the Paris Agreement. Similar lobbying-related successes have been reached at dozens of other companies. Some, such as those against ConEd and ConocoPhillips, were withdrawn prior to voting after management agreed to shareholder demands rather than wage a public battle.

Shareholder proposals in the United States are merely precatory: even if they pass with majority support, a company is not legally required to do what investors want. Still, it is risky for companies to disregard proposals that gain significant shareholder support—even those that fail to reach a majority—because shareholders also hold the power to appoint and remove corporate directors and vote against compensation packages of executives who haven't done their bidding. In a striking report released in July, BlackRock revealed that it had voted against 53 different companies for climate-related issues in 2020 and that it had put another 191 companies "on watch," meaning they should be prepared to be voted against in 2021 if they fail to make changes BlackRock has asked of them (behind closed doors). The move now has years of precedent. In 2016, and again in 2020, BlackRock publicized that its votes against the reelection of Exxon board members were motivated by climate concerns. Many investors have supported resolutions for the appointment of board chairs independent from the CEO in cases where chief executives have stubbornly avoided responding to climate demands. Directors ignore their largest shareholder's displeasure at their peril.

What are we to make of this seeming sea change in corporate social responsibility? Critics are correct in pointing out that these measures fall far short of what is needed to avoid catastrophic levels of warming. But to observers of corporate governance, this level of climate activism is unprecedented, almost shocking—and without an analytical vocabulary to make sense of it. The term "activist shareholder" is traditionally used to describe investors, like hedge funds, that buy a sizable stake in one company and press for profit-maximizing changes or a leadership battle at that one company. Instead, what has arisen only very recently is a handful of very large, very diversified, institutional investors pressing for *portfolio-wide* policy changes. BlackRock, for example, has announced it will expect companies to report their climate risks under the framework created by the Financial Stability Board's Task Force on Climate-Related Financial Disclosures (TCFD). (The FSB is an international organization that makes regulatory recommendations to the G20 nations.) Financial regulators around the world have begun requiring that companies disclose their climate risks in accordance with the TCFD. But in the United States, it is not the Securities and Exchange Commission (SEC) that is mandating a new disclosure standard—it's BlackRock.

To understand this recent rise in institutional investor activism, one has to look at the shifting composition of the major players in capital markets over the past decade.

IF YOU'VE BEEN TOLD only one piece of investment advice, it's probably that you should put your money in an index fund. These securities offer a form of "passive" investing: to put it simply, you pay a small fee to a money manager such as Vanguard to buy you a basket of diversified stocks that roughly mirrors the whole economy. If the market (as a whole) goes up, you make money; if it dips, you lose money. By contrast, "active" investing entails paying a money manager to pick stocks for you—to research which are undervalued and are likely to go up—and you pay more for that expertise.

A welter of empirical research over several decades has shown that active managers are bad at their jobs. Individual stock pickers are unlikely to "beat the market" over a typical investor's return horizon. Warren Buffett famously bet a group of hedge fund managers that its stock-picking couldn't beat a passive fund over a ten-year window; he handily won the million-dollar wager. Over time, as this messaging has become more popular—and in particular after the global financial crisis of 2008—people have been pulling their money out of actively managed mutual funds and placing them into passive investments: index funds and exchange-traded funds (ETFs). Because passive funds compete on the fees they charge clients, they benefit from economies of scale. This trend has been one major contributor to rapid concentration of fund providers and what Benjamin Braun has dubbed our new age of "Asset Manager Capitalism": just three firms—BlackRock, Vanguard, and State Street—control 80 percent of the ETF market. BlackRock, which only 16 years ago managed $366 billion in assets, now manages $7.8 trillion. If it were a country, BlackRock would be the tenth wealthiest, after Canada and before Spain. On the average, BlackRock alone controls about 7 percent of every S&P 500 company.

What does all this have to do with climate change? If you own a significant slice of the global economy, you should be very concerned about climate change: damages will likely mount to tens of trillions of dollars by the end of the century. Even if governments fully implement their commitments under the Paris Agreement, the world is nevertheless on track to warm 3–4 degrees Celsius by 2100. At this level of warming, weather events become more frequent and more extreme, disrupting supply chains and destroying infrastructure; workers become less productive; sea levels rise to engulf whole cities; agriculture is severely disrupted; much more energy is required for cooling; and electricity transmission becomes less efficient—to name just a handful of expected effects. Yet within BlackRock's portfolio are many of the fossil fuel–generating companies that are contributing to this crisis. Each year, just one hundred publicly traded companies are responsible for two-thirds of all industrial emissions.

Economist Joseph Stiglitz has labeled the investor practice of collecting short-term profits from companies whose activities will sooner or later be economically devastating as a type of institutional schizophrenia. Recent institutional investor activism on the climate suggests that money managers are finally waking up to this internal conflict within their portfolios. Shareholders have increasingly been battling management on an array of issues: stopping anti–carbon regulation lobbying, reducing capital expenditures on the exploration and development of fossil reserves, and releasing analysis on just how well their business would fare in a world that successfully limits warming to 2 degrees Celsius. And asset managers admit they are applying pressure on individual firms for the benefit of their broader portfolio of investments. A 2019 joint letter signed by many investors, including the California Public Employees' Retirement System and the banking group BNP Paribas, stated that their climate activism against fossil companies was in service to the "value in our portfolios *across all sectors and asset classes*." The multinational bank UBS claims it engages with portfolio firms in order to address "large negative externalities."

But neither corporate governance theory nor real-life corporate regulation has kept pace with this shift in investor perspectives regarding the goal of portfolio maximization. Legal scholarship assumes that the one thing all shareholders have in common is that they desire the maximization of the share price of each individual firm in which they invest. The very norm of so-called "shareholder primacy" rests upon this assumption. Under the theory advanced by Chicago school theorists, shareholders are the "residual claimants" to a firm's assets: they get whatever is left over once a bankrupt firm has paid out its liabilities to all other stakeholders, including suppliers, bond holders, and employee pensions. Therefore, the argument goes, shareholders are the best stewards of corporate objectives. This is why shareholders and no other stakeholders are given various special rights: voting on proxy proposals, approving compensation and mergers, and suing firm leadership on behalf of the corporation itself. Similarly, corporate experts have spent the last three decades arguing that firm managers' performance should be evaluated and rewarded using share price as the primary metric. Paying executives with shares of their own companies, the thinking goes, will align the interests of managers with those of their shareholders, reducing internal "agency costs."

The locus classicus for this view is Milton Friedman's infamous essay "The Social Responsibility of Business Is to Increase Its Profits" (1970). Friedman condemns an executive spending money to reduce pollution beyond the levels required by regulation, calling it "spending someone else's money for a general social interest." But what happens to Friedman's reasoning if these someones are explicitly asking the managers to spend their money on pollution reduction? The law, it turns out, doesn't have a great answer to this question, as the long-reigning concept of shareholder primacy has conflated two ideas into one: maximizing the share price and doing what shareholders want. The new wave of investor behavior over climate change is a striking case in point: when one company's profits are another company's loss but they have the same shareholders, it is wrong to assume these two goals coincide.

This unwinding of the two concepts that make up shareholder primacy has been made even clearer by the Trump administration's efforts to weaken shareholder power in response to climate activism. Pursuant to an executive order on "Promoting Energy Infrastructure," the Department of Labor, which has jurisdiction over retirement funds, issued guidance meant to discourage investment manager engagement with companies on environmental issues. The SEC proposed rules that would make it harder for investors to reissue environmental proposals that failed to receive majority support in prior years. Most significantly, the SEC went out of its way to permit companies to block shareholder proposals entirely, allowing companies to exclude 45 percent of all climate-related proposals from the proxy voting process in 2019. This meant that shareholder proposals at Exxon, Duke Energy, and Chevron requesting the disclosure of emissions reduction targets never even went to a vote.

These changes are not without a constituency. Last summer the Business Roundtable of top U.S. CEOs, including those of oil majors, airlines, car manufacturers, and energy companies, released a much-covered statement *against* shareholder primacy. Since 1997, the letter said, the roundtable had issued corporate governance guidelines indicating that "corporations exist principally to serve their shareholders." In an about-face meant to "supersede" previous statements, the group announced that a corporation's mission is instead to balance the needs of all stakeholders—employees, communities, and shareholders alike—as their "long-term interests are inseparable." Many business commentators interpreted this statement as part of the general shift of public sentiment toward corporate responsibility, one in line with BlackRock's demands for climate risk. But another interpretation is that the roundtable, an organization historically devoted to the interests of executives, is seeking to disempower and ignore shareholders at a time when the largest investors have been pushing an aggressive climate agenda.

The roundtable is not alone. The National Association of Manufacturers has been transparent in its attempts to disempower shareholders of the companies that make up their organization. The trade group funded the creation of the Main Street Investors Coalition, which claims to represent the interests of individual retirees, whose savings, in the hands of large asset managers, are being used for "non-wealth maximizing activism." The coalition argues that votes against fossil companies are motivated by fund managers' personal political beliefs, rather than bottom-line reasons. Now, in this new schema, the accusation of "spending someone else's money for a general social interest" is being made against institutional investors rather than corporate managers. The group has been lobbying for many of the anti-shareholder reforms contemplated by Trump's SEC, even sending fraudulent letters of support from "ordinary Americans" using signatures without permission.

In the 1990s, corporate governance activists Robert Monks and Nell Minow coined the term "universal owner" to describe large investors that are diversified across the entire economy. They have a long-term interest in the health of the economy as a whole, as opposed to the relative performance of any one firm.

The former head of the $1.5 trillion Japanese Government Pension Investment Fund explicitly embraced the term to describe the fund's climate strategy:

> Given our size and long timeframe [our returns are] pretty much dictated by what happens in the overall capital markets, in fact, by what happens to the global economy. . . . [Our fund] is so big it essentially owns the whole investable universe. So, our focus should be on making the whole market better, rather than trying to beat the market.

A sufficiently large portfolio is able to diversify away firm-specific risks, but it remains exposed to systemic ones—risks that broadly affect the entire economy and thus cannot be diminished through diversification, like the Federal Reserve changing interest rates. In the traditional conception of what asset managers do, market risk is taken as a given: they sell you an index fund that mirrors a slice of the market and passively wait for it to go up (or down). But we're entering an entirely new paradigm where one of the most significant sources of economy-wide, non-diversifiable market risk—climate change—is something individual fund managers can influence. Should they be *required* to?

THIS SLOW REALIZATION of the motivations and powers of this new age has left some commentators hopeful. The United Nations, in fact, encourages funds to think like universal owners, and a new nonprofit is considering litigation strategies to force institutional investors to prioritize portfolio growth over individual-firm profits. Describing how several of the world's largest asset managers, including BlackRock and Fidelity, were urging pharmaceuticals companies to collaborate rather than compete on finding a vaccine for COVID-19, popular financial blogger Matt Levine recently mused: "Will the index funds save us?" But there is—of course—a darker side to this newly amassed power. The three largest U.S. asset managers hold an average stake of more than 20 percent of S&P 500 companies. What happens when all competing firms within an industry share the same large shareholders?

In 2014 a trio of economists found that the key players in the U.S. airline industry compete less with one another as a result of being all partially owned by the same institutional investors. In a two-year period, the same seven shareholders who controlled 50 percent of American Airlines's stock also had large ownership shares in American's competitors. This "common ownership" was found to result in higher ticket prices. Since then, similar anti-competitive effects have been found in the banking, pharmaceutical, seed, and even cereal industries.

Institutional investors, of course, deny that they help the firms within their portfolios collude. They insist that they lack the power to influence specific supply and pricing decisions made within firms. When it comes to issues of "corporate social responsibility," however, these same investors are much more willing to trumpet their expectations and influence. At a Federal Trade Commission hearing on common ownership's anti-competitive effects in 2018, BlackRock cofounder Barbara Novick discussed the investor's "engagements" with firms on women's representation on boards, the opioid epidemic, and climate change, but emphasized that discussions were "never about product pricing." But these interventions can and do influence supply and pricing in much the same way as collusive anti-competitive behavior would. The same market power that enables the jacking of airline tickets is key toward making emission reductions happen. Pressuring only a couple oil producers to slash supply is unlikely to have much of an effect on total emissions; their competitors will step in to fill the supply gap. But Climate Action 100+ is targeting, simultaneously, all publicly owned producers and major consumers of fossil products, including auto manufactures and construction companies. And the group is very coordinated in its efforts: individual investor signatories of Climate Action 100+ are tasked with specific companies to pressure, so they share the costs of economy-wide engagement across its membership.

While we may celebrate the ability of institutional investors to combat climate change, or hope that they might address other social ills, we should question the desirability of a democratically unaccountable financial behemoth making centralized resource allocation decisions. This power to control and coordinate product supply across industries implies the market power to harm: to transfer wealth away from workers and consumers with anti-competitive behavior. The rapid growth of asset managers has been likened to the power wielded by trusts in the Gilded Age. Justice William O. Douglas, in a 1948 dissent from the Supreme Court's decision to allow a steel industry merger, argued that the case was at heart about how much power steel executives should be permitted to wield, rather than the immediate economic impacts of the merger. The power to control the economy, he argued, "can be benign or it can be dangerous," but it will "develop into a government in itself" and "should be in the hands of elected representatives of the people, not in the hands of an industrial oligarchy."

Consolidation in the asset management industry shows no signs of slowing, leading some to caution that eventually just twelve funds will control nearly all of corporate America. As corporate governance scholars and activists fight against attempts to weaken institutional investor oversight of corporate managers, we should think harder about the question of who oversees the overseers.

TO SAVE THE CLIMATE, GIVE UP THE DEMAND FOR CONSTANT ELECTRICITY

David McDermott Hughes

MANY DECADES AGO, electricity became the new oxygen, and the vast majority of Americans today believe they need it every moment of every waking or sleeping hour. The United States has built a vast infrastructure for generating, transmitting, and consuming it—all almost entirely based on planet-destroying fossil fuels and nuclear power.

Those fuels hold and store energy. If you accumulate enough of them, you can generate electricity abundantly and reliably. The result is that the average U.S. household uses electric resources far beyond its needs while losing power for fewer than six hours per year. Renewables can provide that plenitude—and already do through wind and solar farms in Texas and California—but not necessarily all the time. The sun shines at us constantly, with more energy than we can possibly use at any moment, but the Earth's rotation puts us in shadow at nightfall. And wind, of course, can simply stop. As a result, the leading fossil- and nuclear-free sources of energy bounce from feast to famine, raising the possibility of more frequent and longer power cuts. Critics—often supporters of natural gas—say wind and solar power are "not ready." Renewables, they warn us, pose an "intermittency problem."

For those seriously concerned about climate change, the inverse —the demand for electrical continuity—may be the real problem. Today's most ambitious plans to abandon fossil fuels—which are certainly not supported by the natural gas industry—allow ten, twenty, or thirty years to wire the whole country with solar and wind power, running all day, every day, for everyone, everywhere. The plans differ in speed, but all agree on the last point: except for six agonizing hours per year, electrons must flow 24/7/365. To make that steadiness possible, solar plants will have to store some electricity during the daytime feast to last through the nocturnal famine. "As economies shift to variable renewables," environmental activist Paul Hawken writes in his aggressive climate proposal *Drawdown* (2017), "management of the power grid with energy storage systems is critical."

But storage means batteries, and battery technology takes time to sell and install. In the case of utility-scale batteries or battery farms, investors have to negotiate with regulators and neighbors. Such friction is impossible to measure now, but additional equipment and infrastructure always create delay. That lost interval—years, in each of the transition scenarios—matters profoundly. Carbon dioxide can trap heat in the atmosphere for 120 years. For the most precarious people, a year's emissions mean the difference between life and death.

So just how critical is continuity, then? And critical for whom? The U.S. grid sends 30 percent of its electricity to residences. As of 2017, 63 percent of those were single-unit, detached dwellings. Under

Hawken's plan in *Drawdown*, these houses will require battery farms and high-tension lines, and until they get them, they will probably draw power from natural gas at night. Thus, each household demanding continuous electricity marginally exacerbates the climate crisis. Perhaps, then, it is critical that we *not* store energy for these houses. At least, we should not do so in a way that hobbles the transition away from fossil fuels. We ought to consider waiting a few years for storage—enduring much more than six hours of downtime every year—for the sake of transitioning more rapidly away from fossil fuels. But few people have championed such residential intermittency. Why not?

SELF-SACRIFICE IS NOT POPULAR, especially at home. After Jimmy Carter suggested we turn down the thermostat in winter, Ronald Reagan banished sweaters to the political graveyard. No one will recommend that we spend the winter being cold. Forgoing the stove for a few hours is a different kind of sacrifice; it doesn't degrade our quality of life so much as reschedule or interrupt activities. Delay is the kindest form of rationing. Yet we are so wedded to availability, predictability, and continuity that any break seems like a sacrifice. Long before the lithium-ion battery, we became addicted to electrical continuity.

This steadiness became normal and expected at home and in the economy when—and precisely because—the home and the economy converged. First, they diverged from a common concept. As developed in the seventeenth century, the term "economy" derives from the Greek word for household or family management (*oikonomos*). Both units rely upon internal cooperation. In the seventeenth and eighteenth centuries, they also ran at roughly the same tempo: when breadwinners slept, so did production and trade. Factories of the Industrial Revolution, however, moved to continuous production. High-energy manufacturing—in blast furnaces, for example—was just too costly to stop and restart. The economy of making goods thus became an insomniac while the family slumbered. Then, for buyers, sellers, and traders of goods, the digital revolution set an alarm clock without snooze. "Business continuity" is now vital—defended from hackers and blackouts alike. So just about every part of the economy outstripped the family completely. The former is always on, whereas the latter—except where someone works the night shift—appears to turn the lights off at night.

In subtle ways, the family has been catching up to the economy. Perhaps the change began in the 1960s when the electric clock replaced the windup alarm. This technology turned an unnoticed midnight blackout into potentially career-wrecking tardiness. Then the digital clock colonized all our appliances, from the TV to the stove: you can't turn them off anymore. If the contractor installs them compactly, you can't even unplug them. Now—through the Internet of Things—they are all going to talk to each other all the time. That will certainly be convenient; houses will run themselves, heating, cooling, and maybe eventually cooking and cleaning through timed algorithms and web-based data. The household will run like always-on, continuous business.

Meanwhile, COVID-19 has forced almost all white-collar workers to telecommute. Thanks to Zoom, meetings have dispersed from the conference room to bedrooms and kitchens. Business continuity now requires uninterrupted electricity in millions of households. For the moment at least, the economy and the family run on the same circuit, and we would seem to need continuity now more than ever. Today's viral interruption, however, may actually teach us how to live with intermittency.

WE WILL CERTAINLY need to be taught. In 2014 the German grid—6 percent of it working on solar energy—only scraped through an eclipse by drawing on other sources of electricity from neighboring countries. The operators saw that one coming. Wind is harder to predict than the sun. In August still air hit California's wind farms during a heat wave, and despite drawing from public and private batteries, the grid still went down in some locales. The more experimental sources of energy—tides, waves, and ocean currents—all vary by hour, season, and forces so mysterious that we call them acts of God. To make matters worse, none of this intermittency coincides with the rhythms of human life. Workers arrive home—where they will cook and turn on appliances—just as the sun is setting, so demand peaks while supply plummets. Many Americans, of course, fall outside this comfortably employed, nine-to-five routine, but the privileged ones who live this way consume enough energy to set the pattern for everyone else. A familiar criticism of solar energy—"Can't store. No power after four."—thus continues to constrain the move from fossil fuels to renewables.

Hughes

Lithium-ion batteries are moving into position to overcome that constraint, but they create problems of their own. Like most form of mining, lithium extraction produces toxins—imposed, in this case, on Indigenous down-winders in Chile. Also like mining, the lithium trade concentrates power and wealth in the hands of few corporations. Sometimes called "bottlenecking," this process converts a resource too plentiful for profit—like sunlight—into a scarce and lucrative commodity. Right now, Tesla seems on track to gain a controlling share of any smart grid connected to electric vehicles; its Powerwall battery is out-competing less toxic technologies, and it could eventually dovetail with software known as "demand response." Through that automated collaboration, your neighbor's car would wash your dishes, but only at night when she doesn't need the former and you can wait for the latter. Google's Nest program will call the shots. A corporate juggernaut is thus taking shape, one that has the power to slow the energy transition and make it less just. Tesla and Google may not have intended to lay the battery trap, but they are now poised to snap it shut.

Storage technologies beyond chemical batteries are either more expensive, more speculative, or both. Solar actually provides one option. Concentrated solar-thermal plants focus sunlight on a vessel of molten salt, heating water to spin a turbine; the salt will hold heat overnight. Unfortunately, the mirrors necessary to build such massive arrays cost a good deal more than conventional photovoltaic panels. Today the world mostly stores bulk energy by pumping water uphill from a lower reservoir to an upper one; this "pumped hydropower" is very efficient but takes a lot of space. A string of reservoirs along the

Appalachians and parallel ones in the Rockies, Cascades, and Sierra Nevada could store power for all our coastal cities, but this idea is not popular—to put it mildly—among conservationists, hikers, and hunters. One can also exploit gravity with a smaller footprint. A train in California dubbed the "Sisyphus Railroad" rides up with excess electricity, and, in periods of low supply, generates electricity as it rolls down. The train cars are very heavy. On the same principle, the startup Energy Vault programs employs cranes to stack and unstack enormous bricks. No one has constructed this device at operational scale. Although the energy of gravity is age old, its storage prototypes are starting from behind.

To succeed, any one of these storage solutions would require the massive financial and political investment of a Green New Deal. We need to make that investment, certainly, in generating and storing renewable energy. But we don't need to slow down the former while the latter catches up. Germany need not remain stuck at 7 percent solar on the grid—its current level of progress—until it can also store 7 percent. Don't restrain a solar farm for the sake of its lagging twin, the battery farm. Of course, hospitals and some industries require continuous power. But some of us—those of us fortunate enough to live in houses—can tolerate intermittency. We can pause the microwave.

IN FACT, planned interruptions already happen elsewhere all the time. They are called "load shedding," and households are the load.

For a stretch in the late 1980s and 1990s, I lived in Harare, Zimbabwe, where the Zimbabwe Electricity Supply Authority (ZESA) brought current to my house. Zimbabweans, many of whom were enjoying their first connection to the grid, used the abbreviation as a synonym for virility. The amount of current depended to a large extent on Kariba hydroelectric dam and reservoir 200 miles away. The dam, in turn, depended on rain in the vast Central African catchment of the Zambezi River. In the 1980s, and probably due to climate change, annual precipitation began to oscillate wildly. When too little rain fell, the Kariba reservoir failed to reach a capacity, and Harare would lack electricity for months. So ZESA planned a rotation among the suburbs. Generally, that meant losing power for half a day per week. The power cut might have been shorter, had people not circumvented it by using their electric stoves immediately before or after. Still, rationing residences allowed hospitals and other essential services to keep running. Only the utility's reputation suffered: ZESA became Zimbabwe Electricity *Sometimes Available.*

Puerto Rico's equivalent agency, the Puerto Rico Electric Power Authority (PREPA), is widely and justifiably ridiculed. In 2018, a year after Hurricane Maria, Puerto Ricans were still attempting to reconstruct the electricity supply. Mountain residents had endured the better part of that year without current, and—even when back on the grid—their power went out unpredictably and alarmingly. When I visited, some activists were hoping to secede from PREPA through community micro-grids. An organization was distributing solar panels—two or so at a time—to the most at-risk, isolated households. The effect would be transformative, said the leader of this effort. I'll call him Raimundo, a pseudonym. Raimundo spoke of "energy independence" and of ending the colonial relationship between Puerto Rico and fossil fuel corporations. Indeed, inhabitants of central Puerto Rico had successfully blocked an oil pipeline some years before. In the grandest vision, the upland could power its own homes and grow its own food too.

Homeowners and residents didn't want the lights to go out, even briefly. The terrain, though, almost invited interruption, and in circumstances far more frequent than hurricanes. The sierra conjoins the variable weather of mountain and island: clouds roll in without warning and midday solar generation drops off. In 2018 such a natural power cut posed no problem for lighting. Charities were already saturating Puerto Rico with "lanterns"—cylindrical devices containing a small panel, LED bulbs, and a USB-rechargeable battery. For everything else, one would need an energy storage device at least as large as a car battery.

"Really?" I asked Raimundo. He gave me a withering look: "A car does not run without a battery." (Actually some diesel engines will start with a push or, if the driver has parked strategically, with a roll downhill.) The battery was, he admitted, "the weak point in the configuration." It would last only seven to ten years and require constant checking. If one drains a battery too low—below 10 to 25 percent, depending on the model—it will die sooner. With the "configuration," one looks with anxiety not at the sun but at the little charge dial on the battery. These problems, Raimundo said, were regrettable but inevitable.

I was not quite convinced. Puerto Ricans need electricity mostly for refrigeration. Food spoils quickly in the tropics, of course. Also, the island's population suffers from a particularly high rate of diabetes; patients need to keep insulin and other medications cool. So, people told me, a fridge needs to run continuously—but, in fact, it doesn't. No appliance that heats or cools runs continuously. Fridges, freezers, air conditioners, and ovens all try to hold a certain temperature against an outside space that is either hotter or colder. If the outside space remained at, say, 75 degrees Fahrenheit—or even if it warmed or chilled at a regular rate—the appliance could run on steady current.

Yet the outside of any oven, room, or house fluctuates unpredictably. Since nature is fickle, the appliance has to fluctuate too—hence the thermostat, which turns your fridge from the low hum of operation to the silence of intermission. With a good seal, your fridge will keep cool during an intermission of three days. (My family made it through Hurricane Sandy on two door-openings per day.) A top-loading fridge works even better. I met a transplanted Minnesotan operating one of these devices in the mountains. At the bottom of the fridge he set the thermostat for 32.5 degrees; the top never heated up beyond 40 degrees. Insulin remains effective even when stored at 46 degrees and will remain viable for four weeks at room temperature. This mountain man found a future with intermittency. "When you solarize your home," he told me, "you have to solarize your life."

Zimbabwe and Puerto Rico thus provide models for what we might call pause-full electricity. Admittedly, neither Zimbabweans nor Puerto Ricans chose to accept this rationing. And in Zimbabwe, official incompetence has reduced electricity to a nearly unbearable degree. Still,

Zimbabwe's past and Puerto Rico's potential indicate just and feasible ways of living amid intermittency. With a pause, life goes on. By abiding that interlude—by shedding their load—people can preserve life near and far. If my town's blackout will lessen, say, the force of Puerto Rico's next hurricane, then, please, shed us half a day per week.

COVID-19 HAS PULLED BACK THE CURTAIN on inequality and racism in the United States. Less dramatically, it has shown us our obsession with continuity. Take the oil industry. ExxonMobil and other supermajors invest billions of dollars to make sure that oil and gas ship from their underground warehouses continuously. Only occasionally have oil executives wondered what would happen if consumers stopped buying their product. They labeled this unlikely event "demand destruction" and laughed at the endeavors of Greta Thunberg and the anti–fossil fuel movement. They were thus totally unprepared for the demand-destroying global lockdown in March. Pipelines kept pumping, oil accumulated at terminals and tanks, and—for one crazy day in April—sellers would pay buyers just to take it off their hands. They had oversupplied the market. The injunction "Drill, baby, drill!" was predicated on the assumption of nearly constant demand, without intermission.

Now the pandemic has interrupted everything and cut many lives short. Though some societies—notably New Zealand—are still relatively secure, no one knows how long this will last. With the possibility of a new wave this winter and further viral recurrences, commerce may not run smoothly for quite some time. Many have already adjusted to shortages and rationing of basic goods, from beans to toilet paper. To explain that kind of intermittent economy, some politicians have lately been reaching for an unlikely metaphor: inconstant electricity. They describe the slow, trial-and-error re-opening of restaurants, schools, and businesses as turning a dimmer. The economic lights will not simply spring on; they will flicker as disease rises and falls. No one wants to lives this way, of course. But responsible leadership must be prepared to dim the economy with shelter-in-place orders—if not in Washington, then in Wellington. When required for safety, interruption means survival and life.

What applies in the pandemic also applies—and also with desperate urgency—in the climate crisis. We can live with some intermittency and rationing—at least until batteries and other forms of energy storage are up and running everywhere. Hospitals certainly need 100 percent reliable equipment—perhaps some "continuous" businesses and cell towers too. And in cities, elevators, streetlights, and subways must run reliably. One could imagine battery-assisted, semi-smart micro-grids connecting such infrastructure as well as home medical devices. But we don't need the entire residential third of U.S. electricity consumption to run off lithium or to operate seamlessly. We don't need Nest or permanent telecommuting. For a while, let's eat a cold dinner here and there. Continuity costs too much. Climate change kills, and it kills vulnerable people first. In-termittency saves lives, and it saves vulnerable people first. Let the pause take its place in continuous climate activism.

THE TROUBLE WITH CARBON PRICING
Matto Mildenberger & Leah C. Stokes

OVER A DECADE AGO, California put a price on carbon pollution. At first glance the policy appears to be a success: since it began in 2013, emissions have declined by more than 8 percent. Today the program manages 85 percent of the state's carbon pollution and has been lauded as the best-designed carbon pricing program in the world.

But while the policy looks good on paper, in practice it has proven weak. Since 2013 the annual supply of pollution permits has been consistently higher than overall pollution. As a result, the price to pollute is low, and likely to remain that way for another decade. This slack in the system has made the policy better at revenue collection than at changing corporate behavior.

This is not a surprise. Though legislators aimed to tighten the law in 2017, oil and gas lobbyists thwarted their efforts. One powerful labor union initially supported ending free permits for big polluters, but reversed its position after Chevron offered it a union contract to retrofit refineries. The final legislation prohibited enacting new regulations on California's fossil fuel industry—regulations that could have done more than the state's weak carbon price. Even in one of the most progressive environmental jurisdictions in the world, California lawmakers failed to secure the necessary reforms for effective carbon pricing. Rather than carbon pricing, other regulations—clean electricity standards, clean car programs, and aggressive energy efficiency—deserve much of the credit for the state's progress.

California is one of only twelve U.S. states to have adopted any carbon price—the idea has simply proven difficult to enact. When Oregon attempted to vote on a carbon pricing bill in 2019, Republican legislators fled the state and hid in Idaho to prevent the quorum necessary to pass the law. And this isn't just happening in the United States—the policy is politically unpopular around the world. When Australia passed a modest carbon tax in 2011, things got ugly quickly: right-wing radio hosts hurled misogynistic invectives against Prime Minister Julia Gillard; angry protesters descended on the parliament building in Canberra; and climate-denying opposition leader Tony Abbott crisscrossed the country, accusing the government of "economic vandalism." When he took office three years later, Abbott quickly repealed the policy. In France a proposed carbon tax fueled the country's yellow vest movement, triggering the worst domestic riots since 1968. The proposal was soon abandoned.

Despite its political deficiencies, carbon pricing has dominated climate policy conversations for three decades. Part of its enduring appeal is that it provides an elegant response to a complex problem. Carbon pollution is everywhere. So, economists argue, increase the cost of releasing it into the atmosphere, and let markets take care of the rest.

This may be the optimal economic policy for reducing carbon pollution, but as the centerpiece of climate reforms, it has proven a political disaster. As political scientist Jessica Green argues, the policy has done "more harm than good." It highlights the short-term costs of climate action, jacking up the public's energy bills, while concealing the long-term benefits of addressing climate change—for the environment, public health, and the economy. This combination of clear, concentrated costs and opaque, diffuse benefits is politically toxic.

Facing coordinated opposition by powerful fossil fuel–aligned interest groups, governments struggle to set the carbon price high or wide enough. When reformers do win—as in California or Australia—they often are forced to compromise on a narrow policy with a low price that fails to cut emissions quickly or deeply enough. Worse still, these reforms may convince both politicians and citizens that the climate crisis has been addressed by giving a false sense that the "problem has been solved."

These well-intentioned half measures also antagonize working people. Fossil fuel companies weaponize growing income inequality, targeting those suffering the most with messages to oppose carbon pricing, even while their corporate business model is left largely untouched. No wonder, then, that polluters increasingly lobby for this solution, often proposing to eliminate regulations in exchange for the carbon price. Beware of fossil fuel companies bearing gifts.

The polluters have understood the basics of climate science for more than fifty years. Rather than using their vast capital to innovate or deploy new technologies, they have funded multibillion-dollar climate denial campaigns since the late 1980s. Even today they continue to propose new fossil gas plants, refineries, and pipelines. Meanwhile climate change continues unabated. The fires that burned the West Coast this summer are a warning of what is to come. If this is what 1 degree Celsius of warming looks like, what will 2 or 3 degrees bring?

To quickly reduce carbon pollution, we must take a bolder approach that centers the politics of climate change. Our preferred solution can be distilled into three words: standards, investments, and justice. To begin, we must set the rules of the road for polluters through standards—timelines for when we must have clean electricity systems, cars, and buildings. We can back these targets and timetables with government investments in both deployment and innovation. Finally, it is essential that we hold polluters accountable and do not leave poor people and people of color behind.

While carbon pricing could play a role in setting standards, any politically viable carbon price won't catalyze pollution reductions across numerous sectors at the necessary pace. Nor will it yield enough revenue to fund commitments such as Joe Biden's promise to spend $500 billion a year on this problem. The window for incremental climate policy has closed. We need climate policy at the scale of the problem.

AS CLIMATE CHANGE RESEARCH grew more prominent in the 1980s, economists described pollution as a "negative externality"—polluters kept the profits from selling fossil fuels while society at large picked up the tab for the harm they caused. If problems such as acid rain were "market failures," then pricing forced polluters to "internalize" the costs. Anyone who released carbon pollution into the atmosphere would have to pay for the harm they caused. Policymakers have consistently pushed this idea at every level since the 1990s. And many economists remain attached to it: over 3,500 U.S. economists, including 27 Nobel laureates, have signed a letter supporting carbon pricing.

The idea developed into two main forms: a carbon tax and cap and trade. Carbon taxes impose a *price* on every unit of carbon pollution released. Cap and trade—also called emissions trading—limits the *quantity* of carbon pollution that can be released, with polluters trading permits to cover their emissions. Both methods promise the same theoretical result: a reduction in pollution.

Like the roots of a tree branching out in search of water, a carbon price would find carbon wherever it was released. Goods made with fossil fuels would rise in cost. In response, people would make a million tiny decisions to get off carbon: buying the electric-powered lawn mower rather than the gas guzzler, jumping on a bicycle for the last mile rather than calling an Uber, switching to an induction stovetop and ditching the fossil gas. And it wouldn't just be the public changing its ways; industries would also find places to cut back on carbon as their cost of doing business rose. Policymakers dreamed of sending these signals out across the economy to coordinate distant actors wherever the messages found them. The government could not possibly regulate all the myriad ways that carbon was emitted, but the power of the market could solve the problem—at least in theory.

The problem with carbon pricing is not the idea on paper—it is its application in practice. According to economists, an effective carbon price must be high enough to make polluters pay for the externalities they generate. It must also cover all economy-wide sources of carbon pollution.

Carbon prices now exist in 46 countries, covering about 22 percent of the carbon pollution that humans release each year. But these policies are riddled with loopholes. New Zealand's cap-and-trade system exempts agriculture, even though agriculture is responsible for over half of the nation's emissions. Mexico has a small carbon tax on fossil fuel production that excludes fossil gas completely. And in the United States, 11 out of 12 states with any carbon price only apply it to the power sector.

Big carbon polluters—fossil fuel companies, electric utilities, automakers, petrochemical companies, and other heavy industries —have used their structural power to receive policy exemptions, handcuffing the invisible hand of carbon pricing. The result is that carbon pricing passes in the places that already have little pollution. For example, all U.S. states with carbon pricing already had below average per capita energy-related carbon pollution in 2006, before these policies came into effect. Rather than reaching all parts of the economy, carbon prices across the world pick which industries have to pay for pollution and which get a free ride.

Even when prices do exist, they are quite low. According to the World Bank, countries need policies between $40 to $80 per tonne to meet the Paris Agreement targets. Yet half of the world's carbon prices are less than $10 per tonne, while only five countries—Sweden,

Norway, Liechtenstein, Switzerland, and France—are in the target range. Even the prices in these countries are probably too low. Estimates for the social cost of carbon—a measure of the societal harm carbon pollution causes—range from a couple dozen to several hundred dollars per tonne of CO_2. University of California San Diego climate scientist Kate Ricke and colleagues estimate this social cost could be a staggering $417 per tonne. No carbon price in the world comes close to that number.

Nor are the handful of high carbon prices unambiguous successes. In Norway, which has one of the highest carbon prices in the world, emissions in the oil sector rose by 78 percent between 1990 and 2017. One reason emissions didn't fall is because of a problem economists call "demand inelasticity": if an economic activity is extremely profitable, or if there are no easy alternatives, people and companies may not demand less even as prices increase. Economists Geoffrey Heal and Wolfram Schlenker argue that high carbon taxes won't effectively reduce pollution unless cheap substitute technologies are available.

The evidence is mixed, however, on whether carbon prices can drive innovation and provide more of these cheaper substitutes we need. In her study of the national U.S. cap-and-trade program for sulfur dioxide, Margaret Taylor found that innovation actually declined after the system went into effect. As Tobias Schmidt has shown, cap-and-trade systems tend to produce incremental improvements in polluting technologies rather than driving new, clean alternatives.

Other research suggests limited innovation. In their study of the EU's carbon market, economists Raphael Calel and Antoine Dechezleprêtre estimate that patenting increased by 9 percent for regulated firms. However, given how few companies fell under the carbon price, overall low carbon technology patenting increased by less than 1 percent. Carbon price–induced patenting in the UK may have been considerably higher. Still, we lack strong evidence that carbon pricing has rapidly induced the innovation we need in new, cleaner technologies. By focusing on the low-hanging fruit—the "cheapest" ways to cut carbon pollution—we fail to build the ladder necessary to curb the more difficult emissions to reduce.

And that shouldn't surprise us. Consider this scenario: if the United States managed to implement a $50 per tonne carbon price, gasoline prices would increase by $0.44 per gallon. That means Americans' monthly driving costs would increase by about $25, enough to put a dent in many families' budgets. Some people might drive a bit less; a few might set up a carpool. But corporations will not innovate new technology because of minor tweaks in the price of energy. The prices of oil already fluctuate greatly year to year, and that hasn't exactly produced the climate technology we need. Fossil fuel companies spend next to nothing on clean energy innovation and deployment.

If it hasn't driven the necessary innovation, perhaps carbon pricing has delivered emission cuts? That's a tough question to answer, given pollution's tight link to GDP. During the financial crisis, global carbon pollution levels declined by 1.4 percent between 2008 and 2009 before rebounding. This was not the result of government policy, but that of an economic downturn. We see a similar trend now during the COVID-19 pandemic. Global carbon pollution is estimated to fall by a record 4–7 percent in 2020 as a result of the economic slowdown. But these reductions will be temporary in the absence of ambitious climate reforms.

Evaluations of carbon pricing require models that make assumptions about the way the world would have unfolded if the policy hadn't passed—what we call "business as usual" scenarios. One model suggests Norway's carbon tax reduced carbon pollution by about 2 percent in its first decade. Similarly the EU cap-and-trade system likely reduced emissions by about 4 percent between 2008 and 2016. In British Columbia, Canada, the carbon tax may have been more successful, reducing emissions by 5–15 percent between 2008 and 2015. But these reductions, while laudable, are nothing compared to what needs to be done—we need annual cuts of almost 8 percent a year until 2030 to limit warming to 1.5 degrees Celsius.

Evidence suggests carbon pricing won't drive emissions reductions quickly enough. It is like bringing a stick to a knife fight. The policy might help for a little while, but it's unlikely to secure a victory without other weapons to attack the problem. Economists have tried to sharpen the stick, pushing for better policy design, higher prices, and broader coverage. But their efforts have largely failed. To understand why, we need to dig deeper into the *politics* of carbon pricing.

AS A POLICY, carbon pricing has the politics backward. It starts by changing the incentives to pollute. Theoretically these incentives will undermine carbon polluters' economic and political power. But this puts the cart before the horse: we need to disrupt the political power of carbon polluters *before* we can meaningfully reshape economic incentives.

The policy also makes it easy for fossil fuel companies to rally opposition. Presenting themselves as champions of the little guy, these companies highlight how the policy would increase gasoline and electricity costs for the public. Polluters have even helped school boards and local governments estimate impacts from a carbon tax on their budgets. It's not difficult to draw attention to these costs when everywhere we drive, giant signs declare the price of gasoline. If that number rises, people notice. There are no roadside signs displaying the devastating costs of climate change: wildfires, stronger hurricanes, rising sea levels, and new infectious diseases such as COVID-19.

What if we could make the benefits of carbon pricing more visible? This is the logic behind the price-and-dividend approach. Canada and Switzerland are the only two countries that have adopted this policy, though it is also part of proposed legislation in Congress. Like traditional cap and trade, this policy would cap emissions and require that companies buy pollution permits. Then U.S. residents with Social Security numbers would receive money back from the program, gathered from polluting firms. According to political scientist Theda Skocpol, a dividend would give the public a tangible benefit to organize around, thus contesting the power that entrenched polluters have over U.S. policymaking. Give the public a green check every month, the thinking goes, and it might just embrace climate policies.

This is especially true for low-income households. Recent models by economists Anders Fremstad and Mark Paul show that a

U.S. carbon tax, without compensation, would impose the greatest burdens on low-income households. A dividend could be designed to disproportionately return revenues to poor households.

Carbon price and dividend gives greater attention to the politics of climate policy than earlier approaches, but it still struggles to make the benefits more salient than the costs. In the two countries with a price and dividend, the benefits are buried in income tax or health insurance forms. In our own research, we find these policies do not substantively increase public support for climate policy. This shouldn't surprise us. Dividends are, at best, a band-aid solution to carbon pricing's political woes. They create a debate over whether people want a check to cover their increased energy costs. Yes, some would rather have the check, but most would still prefer cheap energy.

Carbon pricing may cut pollution in economists' models. But these models do not include a clear political pathway to turn their results into reality. The idea may be better suited for later stages in society's decarbonization efforts, to help optimize carbon pollution reduction at the margins. But as a short-term political strategy, it's deeply flawed.

WE NEED TO BE THINKING at least as hard about the politics of climate policy as we are about economic efficiency. Climate policy is a repeated game unfolding over decades. Any meaningful approach must build political allies as it weakens the fossil fuel industry. To cultivate the advocates necessary for more ambitious action, we need to grow our clean energy industries—and fast. If we want 100 percent clean electricity by 2035 in the United States, we need to deploy clean energy technologies around 4 times faster than we have in the past. This speed cannot be achieved through carbon pricing alone.

Achieving this pace requires a different suite of policies, including a clean electricity standard, streamlined permitting, and government investments. Unlike carbon pricing, clean electricity standards already exist in most states and are driving progress, growing the political allies necessary to secure federal action. In late 2020 Google made the bold announcement that it would target 100 percent clean electricity by 2030, delivered 24 hours a day, 7 days a week to all its facilities. What might happen if this powerful company, which is also one of the top electricity consumers in the country, lobbied for a federal clean electricity law?

Progress also requires taking inequality seriously. We cannot raise the cost of energy for millions of underpaid Americans—many of whom are Black and Indigenous—and expect the policy to stick. We need to know that when it comes time to impose stiffer costs on polluters, perhaps through a carbon tax, cheaper technologies will be available to ensure that everyone can afford to swap out their appliances. The policy goal should be to ensure that when any furnace, stove, car, or power plant comes to the end of its life, it is replaced by a low-carbon option. This will also make the transition cheaper, as we won't reinvest in carbon polluting infrastructure that we need to discard early. We should be thinking: what policies will make the default choice the clean choice?

To make this happen, the government should spend trillions of dollars on clean energy in the coming decade. By investing in new clean energy projects, rather than imposing costs on existing assets through a carbon tax, economists Julie Rozenberg, Adrien Vogt-Schilb, and Stéphane Hallegatte suggest that the world can decarbonize without triggering a backlash through asset value destruction. In truth we may have to pay, rather than tax, to get rid of polluting assets, perhaps through loans that are conditional on deploying clean technology. Similarly, the government should make a clear plan for fossil fuel industry workers. We can't allow this transition to hobble workers while fossil fuel executives deploy golden parachutes before declaring bankruptcy and laying everyone off.

The objective should not be getting "the prices right," but passing large-scale industrial policy that steers our society where we need to go. The good news is that Biden has already committed to this approach. And these plans are surprisingly popular, even among Republicans. According to our research, at least three-quarters of Republican voters in every congressional district support funding renewable energy research. The lesson here is that we can build successful political coalitions around climate policy when we give people something to fight *for*. If jobs and benefits are front and center, support for action will follow.

To get these policies passed, we'll need our justice system to hold polluters accountable. The courts have become a key venue for challenging the fossil fuel industry's social license to pollute with impunity. Modeled after the successful challenges to the tobacco industry, this approach has three prongs: first, using the Racketeer

Influenced and Corrupt Organizations Act (RICO) to sue companies such as Exxon for climate denial and for misleading shareholders; second, public nuisance cases against fossil fuel companies and electric utilities; and third, strict regulatory enforcement.

Lawsuits are already underway in several states, with similar court cases playing out in countries across the globe, including from children plaintiffs arguing that governments are neglecting to protect them. These lawsuits are promising. Even if climate advocates do not win every case, legal attacks can induce what Jacob Hacker and Paul Pierson call "strategic accommodation," wherein policy opponents champion costly policies to forestall even worse outcomes. With the threat of never-ending legal battles on the table, fossil fuel corporations may finally be willing to negotiate a meaningful climate deal.

Credible legal threats could also pull the Republican Party back from the brink of climate denial. Faced with the prospect of both a Green New Deal *and* legal attacks on big fossil fuel polluters, some Republicans have decided to wake up and throw their weight behind more "reasonable" approaches. Proposals, backed by the fossil fuel industry and some Republicans, have included trading a carbon tax for immunity from tort lawsuits or weakened regulations. Taking those trades would have been a terrible deal for climate activists, but the offer shows just how effective these court cases can be.

With strong regulatory enforcement, executive action also has a role to play. Under the Obama administration, the Clean Air Act was used to regulate carbon pollution from new and existing power plants. In the late 1990s, the Clinton administration filed almost two dozen lawsuits against utility companies, claiming they had made serious facility changes under the cover of routine maintenance without requesting appropriate EPA reviews. In most of these cases, utility companies settled with the government, agreeing to pay billions in cleanup costs.

Carbon pricing ignores all of these strategies because it ignores political power. Economists argue that because all molecules of carbon pollution are identical, we should eliminate the easiest and cheapest pollution sources first. But it is more politically powerful to shut down a coal plant than it is to have everyone turn off their lights more often.

THE TIME FOR INCREMENTAL climate policy has passed. If the United States had adopted a carbon price in 1990, we would be in a very different world today. But fossil fuel companies and other big polluters resisted this approach. Instead of changing their business model, they spent billions funding climate denial and delaying government efforts to address the growing crisis.

The hour grows late and we find ourselves on the losing side of the battle. Carbon concentrations are now at a level unseen since humans first walked the Earth. Fires have ripped across Australia and North America this year at unprecedented scales. We have run out of letters for the hurricanes this season. Some scientists believe the Greenland ice sheet has melted past the point of no return. Climate change is happening now. And it is scarier than we anticipated.

We must respond at the scale of this crisis—and this necessitates breaking fossil fuel companies' stranglehold on our political system. Once we realize this, we can focus on the weapons we need in battle: new political allies—cultivated through large-scale industrial policy—and strategic lawsuits and regulations, to bring polluters to the table. Economists may have to kill their darling carbon price, beautiful on paper and woefully problematic in practice.

But this doesn't mean that they must abandon their principles. As many economists argue, their models suggest that a clean electricity standard and a carbon price are similar from an economic perspective. Yet politically this is not true. Setting a clear target for clean energy centers the benefits of action. It says: we will make a market for good things. We will create jobs. We will make progress. A carbon price's primary political message is: we will make you pay for doing bad things. And the amount of benefits it might provide is unclear to most people.

Economists and climate policymakers must ask themselves: Is insistence on theoretical efficiency more important than delivering climate stability? This crisis demands pragmatism. We must make the benefits clear, through standards, investments, and justice that hold polluters accountable. Let's pass a federal law at the scale of the crisis and one that will stick. We cannot afford to wait another decade.

THIS VEIL OF SMOKE
Erica X Eisen

STEPPING OUT OF my apartment building in southern Bishkek one cold November morning in 2019, I was met with a smell that I immediately recognized as fire. I had grown up in southern California, remembered drought-spawned chaparral blazes that would leap over highways and engulf whole tracts of housing, closing schools for a week at a time as waves of people fled for the safety of the coast. I remembered a red sun, a grey sky, a rain of ash, and above all else the acrid smell that closed around me now.

But scrolling through news site after news site revealed nothing: no warehouse gone up in smoke, no stray spark from an electrical wire. The men and women who walked past me did so unhurriedly, without panic, seeming not to register the scent of the air, the smudgy sky. Still unsure, I crossed the street to the weekend bazaar, which bustled as usual with butchers, fishmongers, and vegetable sellers all calmly bagging produce and doling out change. I picked some potatoes from a tarp, some carrots from a cardboard box. When I returned home, I realized that the smell was on my clothes, my hair, my skin. In the ensuing hours and days, it would come to leak into the apartment itself, and then I stopped noticing it, and life, as it always does, went on.

AT VARIOUS POINTS throughout this past winter, the Kyrgyz capital of Bishkek topped air quality charts as the city with the worst pollution in the world. Visitors have been warned away, residents discouraged from leaving home without a mask. Photos taken from the slopes that ring the city disclose an eerie sight: no rooftops, no towers, just an all-engulfing lake of smog.

Begun as a mud-walled fort to allow the Uzbek Khanate of Kokand to more easily tax and control traders in this corner of their empire, Bishkek grew in importance after the Russian conquest, first as a Cossack waystation and then, after the revolution, as the capital of the Kara-Kirghiz Autonomous Oblast in freshly carved-up Turkestan. Under Soviet rule, the newly minted capital earned renown as the greenest city in Central Asia, its parks numerous, its boulevards stately and tree-shaded, its botanical gardens meticulously laid out by scientists from across the Eastern Bloc. But after the collapse of the USSR, the city's population ballooned, increasingly placing public greenery under the axes of developers. Cars, so rare during Soviet times that drives were a treat reserved for wedding parties, became mainstays of daily life, flooding the pedestrian-oriented streets with ten times the number of vehicles they were designed to contain. As the winter chill descends, car exhaust combines with the smoke of coal burnt for heat and lies quiltlike over the city as though pinned in place during long windless stretches. What I was smelling on my first truly cold day in Kyrgyzstan was a reality to which native Bishkekers have been forced to acclimate over the last several years. And I was unprepared for how radically it would rework my experience of the city.

To live beneath this veil of smoke is also to unlive, to feel that life even more than usual is interwoven with its opposite. It is to see the stitches of my routines unpicked one by one as the healthy is transformed into the harmful, the pure into the putrid. *Are you exercising?* a friend writes to me in a solicitous email. I am not: health officials have announced that Bishkek residents should refrain from any strenuous physical activity that might elevate their breathing rate. One of the city coroners, so I heard, has said that among the bodies of smokers and nonsmokers in the Bishkek morgue, there is no difference: the same black lungs.

During the worst stretches, it is as though my life has been pared down to a point: the walk to the university, to the market, home. In between, stretches of space that to my imagination now seem impossibly vast, obstacles separating me from sealed reservoirs of clean air. Perhaps others feel this way as well; perhaps it is for this reason that the rhythms of life in Bishkek's air crisis are palpable as much online as in the flesh. In Facebook groups, on Twitter, the air becomes an all-encompassing obsession, the beginning and end, it sometimes seems, of every conversation. We watch as pollutant figures tick up and down with the hours and days and weeks, rising and ebbing like the moon-pulled tides. We discern patterns, augur future trends. We trade home fixes like grandmothers swapping recipes for lemon curd or tricks for rubbing out a stain. Would wrapping your scarf around your face help? What about wrapping it twice? We debate which metric to use, which data to trust. The monitoring sites are a language whose grammar I memorize alongside Russian cases and reflexive verbs: red for merely unhealthy, a muddy purple—which Bishkek has been reaching more and more—for hazardous. The numbers and graphs give our subjective experiences the solidity and comfort of the definite, something more concrete and defined than the heavy feeling in our lungs. There is nothing we can do. But at least we can understand.

THEY CALL IT "the heating season": the long stretch when the temperatures drop low enough that life without a radiator would be intolerable. For those on Bishkek's periphery, however, out where the military-straight lines of the center's streets fracture and fray into dirt roads lined with jerrybuilt housing, the precipitous descent into winter means months spent eking out what warmth can be gotten from burning coal, garbage, rags.

The collapse of collective farms at the end of the Soviet era ushered in a wave of capital-bound migration from the countryside areas most Kyrgyz simply call "The Regions." Shut out of formal housing, many of these migrants were forced to take up residence in one of the so-called "new builds" that have cropped up around the city, informal settlements that the city largely refuses to grant legal status. Without official recognition, many of these neighborhoods lack access to electricity, health services, running water, the right to vote in municipal elections—and gas. However bad it is, the smog I breathe on my walk to and from the university where I work is nevertheless a pale version of what must be endured by those who must burn coal in their homes in order to survive the winter.

Ask anyone in Bishkek about the pollution and they'll give you two reasons for it: the cars and the coal. But the conversation usually hits a wall there, with no inquiry into *why* the city's poor must resort to burning coal in the first place. It's hard not to sense here something of the disdain native Bishkekers express for migrants all the time: *They don't speak Russian. They drive like maniacs. They have hulking cars meant to carry sheep.* For such people, the pall in the air is but another manifestation of the spiritual contamination inflicted by these newcomers upon the lost capital of their Soviet youth, once so stately, once so fine, whose tea shops and shaded walks they now can visit only in their dreams.

THE LADIES IN THE POLLUTION MASK ADS are all white. They smile, they smolder, they pout, eyes so intense it is easy to forget that their faces are half hidden. In the capable hands of the mask-ad ladies, a utilitarian piece of safety equipment has morphed into something sleeker, softer, a canvas for infinite stylistic variations. There are masks in camo, in gingham, in springtime florals, in every color under the sun; there are masks with printed-on grins and moustaches and cartoonish tendrils of drool. They inhabit a strange universe, these mask-ad ladies, wearing award show–ready unsmudgeable makeup and staring out from frames in which nothing at all exists, no worries or cares, no illness, and certainly no smoke.

The idea that we all breathe the same air has become something of a hackneyed staple of appeals for political unity. But around me I see it very clearly: breath is something, increasingly, that you can buy. The optimist's fond belief that a "we're all in the same boat" practicality will prevail when it comes to galvanizing around environmental issues is deeply misplaced: safety and comfort—or at least their illusion—will always be available to the highest bidder. In a city such as Bishkek, where the environmental crisis is so deeply rooted in governmental rot, perhaps what the mask advertisements sell more than anything else is the opportunity to pretend, even a little bit, that the state around us is functioning. The mask-ad ladies do not have to walk past burning trash on the way to the store. They do not have to fill their cars with low-grade smuggled gasoline, and they certainly would never stoop to bribing their way past a smog check. No: theirs is a good world, a clean world, a world which anyone can enter for a price. Walking past a trendy coffee shop one day, I notice that it has begun selling air purifiers, sleek white boxes that promise to sanitize your home once you park them in the corner of your living room. The ads show interiors speckled with potted plants, handwoven baskets, furniture rendered in smooth Scandinavian wood. The light is soft, the walls are white, and everything looks pure pure pure. If you bought one, if you turned it on and closed your eyes, would you think you were elsewhere?

THE WAY YOU FEEL IT: how the air here is not a void but something to be seen and smelled and tasted, an acid sting etching itself into the inside of your mouth on the days when the pollution is at its worst. The way it comes in like an uninvited guest, its particles insinuating themselves under doors and between the gaps in window insulation to lie upon everything in a fine, filthy dust you could write in with your finger. But there is an important sense in which the pollution we live with in Bishkek becomes a pollution of the heart. It's the realization, as I prepare for a visit to my mother in America, that I have not one item of clothing that does not smell of ash. It is in the paranoia with which I regard every lingering cough as a possible symptom of something worse. Above all else, it is the numbness of normality that settles in before long, the feeling that this is a fixed and immutable part of life here, how things are and always will be, and it is the fight against this feeling, the everyday struggle to remember the fire beneath the smoke.

Eisen

THE POLITICS OF THE ANTHROPOCENE IN A WORLD AFTER NEOLIBERALISM

Duncan Kelly

HISTORIAN ADAM TOOZE has argued that COVID-19 is the first economic crisis of the *Anthropocene*, a term encapsulating the idea that human impact on the environment and climate is so extreme that it has moved us out of the Holocene into a new geological epoch. While this argument remains the subject of deep disagreement among experts, those advocating for the Anthropocene emphasize that humans have so drastically altered the environment that we have become agents of transformations we cannot reliably control. Indeed, we are daily reminded of these effects by extreme weather events, species extinctions, and new global health emergencies.

The most pressing and most obvious of these forces is the novel coronavirus, which has exposed the frailties of political systems in so-called advanced democracies in collectively terrifying but individually unsurprising ways. As with other pandemics, the least powerful and most insecure members of society are those who suffer the most. If one of the challenges posed by the Anthropocene is to rethink the evaluative and ecological foundations of our politics in dramatic new ways, it might help to make better sense of the challenges we face—and to build a better and fairer world after neoliberalism—to explore the convoluted route by which we have arrived at this point. The pandemic struck at a moment of deep-seated disaffection with democratic politics after forty years of neoliberalism and the rise of new forms of authoritarian and populist politics.

Facing his own era-defining political crisis, German chancellor Gustav Stresemann (1878–1929) took the title of a 1920 silent film starring Bela Lugosi, *Dance on the Volcano*, and turned it into a serious metaphor by which to describe the economic threats faced amid the rise and decline of the Weimar Republic—from military defeat and a quietly successful democratic revolution to economic catastrophe, militaristic nationalism, and rising anti-Semitism. While the early 2020s are certainly not the late 1930s, the metaphor remains convincing.

Can today's crises inspire action at the scales required to think about planetary sustainability? Why has it proven so difficult politically to act in the face of ample evidence of an increasingly uninhabitable Earth, to which now can be added the threat of COVID-19?

DURING THE PANDEMIC, Tooze has disinterred German sociologist Ulrich Beck as an unlikely Virgil to guide us through this uncertain modern purgatory. Beck's thinking about what he termed "risk society" seems even more pertinent during an Anthropocene pandemic than it did thirty-five years ago.

Kelly

Reflecting on environmental fallout, Chernobyl, and ecological politics in 1980s Germany, Beck asked what it meant to live amidst the new risks of modern society—from disease and radioactive fallout to still broader forms of ecological calamity. How, he wondered in *Risk Society* (1986), can we "live on the volcano of civilization without deliberately forgetting about it, but also without suffocating on the fears" that erupt from within? This combination of scientific knowledge of threats, alongside a fear of the invisible agency of both viral and radioactive hazards, offers a perverse combination of hypermodernism amid a sort of quasi-religious fear and primitivism around the unseen. Such an unstable compound formed part of Beck's search for a more "reflexive" form of modernization. As he put it in *Ecological Politics in an Age of Risk* (1995), society in the age of climate crisis—when we are "confronted by the challenges of the self-created possibility, hidden at first, then increasingly apparent, of the self-destruction of all life on this earth"—passes through two stages.

The first offers technocratic solutionism, grounded in models of economic growth and progress, which allows modern experts something like "wardship" of Earth. And while democracy might "twitch" at moments of mismanagement by technocrats, it can do so only after its practical "demise" as a political force in the first place. During this stage, all trends point toward ever greater power in the hands of unelected experts, while democracy continues to function as an ideological illusion—a spell cast over the world by a word only loosely connected to how power is exercised in day-to-day politics.

The second stage of risk society, what Beck termed "hazard civilization," takes place at the level of knowledge production. As we become increasingly aware of the fragility of our situation and the proximity of existential risks and hazards, we obviously become more and more beholden to experts for understanding and surviving the threats they have done so much to inform us about. Yet at the same time that they offer complex and rarefied knowledge about problems that threaten our collective existence, scientists and experts show—in full view of the public—the powerful disagreements, divergences, and dissonance among themselves in the production and distribution of expert claims. Just think of the politicking behind the massive documents and appendices of the 2018 report by the Intergovernmental Panel on Climate Change, which focused on the need to keep future warming within 1.5 degrees Celsius. In turn it quickly became a rallying cry, taken up particularly by those on the frontline of climate change in the Caribbean, suggesting that this was really about "1.5 to stay alive."

As figures such as Bruno Latour have emphasized, increased awareness of science as an argumentative social practice and continuous process of negotiation and interpretation serves two conflicting functions. On the one hand, it provides intellectual emancipation from ignorance: recognizing complexity and uncertainty is a form of liberation. But on the other hand, it also breeds skepticism about scientific knowledge. This can, in turn, make possible reactionary forms of critique, quickly taken up by institutions and ideologies seeking to benefit from the status quo. Such a state of affairs leaves us even further adrift, for the insidious threats of risk society and hazard civilization are also social and massively unequally distributed. As Beck wrote, in the face of massive hazards and existential threat, what use is a society that protects individuals in their acquisition of extreme wealth and that legitimates massive levels of income and wealth inequality through property rights at the same time that it "legalizes large-scale hazards on the strength of its own authority, foisting them on everyone, including even those multitudes who resist them"?

In his account of ecological politics in this hazard civilization, Beck paraded the tragedy and irony of atomic modernity as a social structure of "non-liability." Its distinctive features lay in "turning that which controls the production of hazards—law, science, administration, policy—into its accomplices." This "theatre of the absurd" in turn "renders all resistance idle," for while it is impossible for society to avoid risk, the "institutionalized safety pledge" social institutions and experts offer interprets the actual presence of hazards as forms of system failure rather than as failures of social relations that have already given themselves over to technocratic management. Social institutions have become "prisoners of their own safety technology," a perverse summation to the solidaristic social-insurance schemes underpinning the original emergence of the modern welfare state.

Beck's alternative vision was to provide space to ground multiple forms of what he called "sub-politics": a return to something like a politics of democratic accountability expressed locally as a form of collective irresponsibility, when set against the paradoxical realities of the new technocracy governing ecological risk. For Beck this was the "antidote" to the pathologies of hazard civilization. But he was deliberately non-stipulative about what direction these forms of politics might take, which makes it sound rather abstract at first. Sub-politics is about fostering spaces for individual and collective political judgment within which local groups and communities can learn to deliberate, think, and act in a world of perpetual risk and hazard—but free from the rigid hierarchies of technical solutionism and an uncritical acceptance of whatever expert knowledge provides as the only justification for political choice-making.

How such processes and places work in practice will have to be determined on the ground, in a bottom-up process of democratic organizing. The politics of organizing has always been crucial to the successes and failures of ecological politics, and for Beck it seems like an activist model of democratic self-government in sub-political perspective is a better antidote to hazard life than the precautionary anti-majoritarianism of some political and constitutional theorizing. Such spaces might also help to avoid the temptation simply to habituate ourselves to a "new normal" with all its abnormalities—as something beyond our control or ken—or to seek solace in the return to earlier times of apparent simplicity and order, with strong leaders and grateful subjects. In the face of current challenges, the search for technological fixes, constitutional amendments, or even forms of constitutional dictatorship may seem emancipatory, but in fact they only bind us to the status quo. They may provide models for salvaging democratic politics tomorrow, but they do so by pre-committing ourselves to contemporary values. What, though, if today is precisely when we need to do things differently?

Others look to a new ethics of interspecies care between kith and kin as a way of "staying with the trouble," in Donna Haraway's terminology. Small wonder, perhaps, that the promise of environmental care and mobilization for the sake of planet Earth and future human

Kelly

generations seem more likely to find a coalition of the willing through nonstate affiliations such as religious groupings, which see themselves as acting above the grubby secular needs of nationalist politics. Amitav Ghosh has laid this out clearly as one way that future historians might look back on this period of failure—one that he calls "the great derangement"—with perhaps a little more sympathy once we recognize the exclusionary nature of a political and economic modernity open only to a relative minority in global terms.

More recently still, proposals for a Green New Deal have offered seemingly novel model political economies, mobilizing groups at both national and what we might think of as various sub-political levels, as well as across generational divides. Yet in so doing, they indicate some of the structural problems connecting the sub-political to the demands of an uninhabitable Earth or a politics of the Anthropocene, which might require a still-more radical rethinking of the very concepts, values, and priorities that underpin modern democratic politics.

For even as such challenges to the mainstream play out and support forms of localism and radical democracy, they often continue to work within the conceptual horizons of a pre-Anthropocene world. Perceiving the urgent need to move beyond forty years of neoliberalism, they hark back—often rhetorically, sometimes substantively—to the allure of the original New Deal. Bypassing the last four decades, we plunge back to forms of Keynesian demand management where government spending, taxation, and plans for full employment in new sustainable jobs are required to finance this transition—meaning a sort of last hurrah for Old World growth and stimulus is the necessary prerequisite for moving into a new world running along a "slower groove," as Kate Aronoff, Alyssa Battistoni, Daniel Aldana Cohen, and Thea Riofrancos put it in *A Planet to Win: Why We Need a Green New Deal* (2019).

Such attempts to revive older models of growth, employment, interest, and money in new forms might not be enough to meet the demands of Beck's challenge. Indeed, it often remains unclear what it might mean to go beyond neoliberalism: there are such diverse understandings of what the term means in theory and practice, and what its history might have to teach us about a future beyond it.

CONSIDER TWO of the most powerfully articulated positions in contemporary scholarship on the topic.

First is the critique of neoliberalism exemplified by Wendy Brown, who sees it as an "undoing" of the demos by self-conscious political choice. Unevenly distributed across the globe, neoliberalism on this account is a "field of oscillations" broadly set upon rendering human interactions and subjectivities into little more than market calculations of individual and comparative advantage. It stealthily weakens any commitment either of individuals or of government to solidaristic ties of affection and mutual aid as beyond the scope of policy-making and detrimental to the acquisition of wealth. Neoliberalism, in this account, is an essentially antidemocratic project: it professes to depoliticize and thereby to naturalize the realm of the economy and of economic competition as the essential measure of human success.

Brown argues, against this regime, that democracy has only ever advanced through the revolt and reforms demanded by the excluded, and it is thus premised on a view of politics grounded in the hope for a better, though perhaps never fully realizable, future. Once a market calculus is applied to democratic politics or to society more broadly, a new kind of political rationality takes hold. Contemporary neoliberalism has conquered a progressive commitment to welfare, offering in its place the simplistic mantra that the state and the economy are separate entities; that the market is smart and rewards according to talent; and that the state is dumb, slow, and corrupted by sinister interests.

For writers such as Neal Ascherson, this suggests that whatever a world beyond COVID-19 looks like, it must surely mean the end of neoliberalism and the affirmation of public goods, not just individual ones. What sort of model of society might that be? As Will Davies recently suggested, democracies in the age of COVID-19 remain stuck between two basic options. One is an imagined community—whether the nationalism of contemporary right-wing populists and the so-called "left behind" or the solidaristic left version—harking back to a better time when communities were close, patriotism was natural, and people looked out for one another's children. The other option is to view society as an amalgam of individuals and groups into vast networks, part of an increasingly interconnected world through forms of technology they might nonetheless remain physically distant from. Its roots lie in the sociological and telecommunications revolutions of the nineteenth century, adapted for a broadband era. Whether mythical, nostalgic, or nodal, such choices still fall victim to the criticisms laid out by Beck.

In contrast to Brown's *political* theory of neoliberalism, a second approach is *historical*. The work of Angus Burgin, Philip Mirowski, and Dieter Plewhe has tracked the roots of modern neoliberalism back to the 1938 conference Colloque Walter Lippmann in Paris and the Mont Pèlerin Society, founded in Switzerland in 1947 by figures including Friedrich Hayek and Milton Friedman. This historical argument emphasizes the organizational effectiveness of an intellectual effort to construct a new liberalism in the wake of war and depression. Intellectual historian Quinn Slobodian extended this argument in his 2018 study *Globalists*, which recasts the origins of neoliberalism as an attempt to shift political power away from nation-states toward supranational federal architectures—from the League of Nations to the World Trade Organization. This vision began life as a sort of updated Habsburg Empire model, wherein cultural diversity could thrive under political structures too complex to be captured by bureaucratic or national interests. (Hayek and his teacher Ludwig von Mises saw World War I as a calamitous triumph of nationalism and socialism within the modern nation-state.)

Such complex, supranational structures were once thought to be among the best ways to save capitalism not only from itself, but from the distortions of statist politics. Neoliberal versions of this history were a capitalist mirror to wider, anticolonial critiques of the nation-state that developed at the same time. But what trajectories link the historical dynamics of the modern statist politics that won out against these competing visions into the uninhabitable Earth of the Anthropocene?

Kelly

In *Climate Leviathan* (2018), Geoff Mann and Joel Wainwright give a typology of various political structures that might emerge in response to climate change. One option is "Climate Leviathan," a system of global capitalism premised upon the already wealthy and powerful being motivated to save the planet for their own interests. Another vision is "Climate Mao," which responds to the climate crisis not by global capitalism but by seemingly anti-capitalist and autarchic blocs. Still another option is "Climate Behemoth," a reform of reactionary populism at the level of the nation-state. But beyond these options, Mann and Wainwright contend, we might also imagine some sort of Climate X, a radical democratic rethink of the forms of sub-national as well as international politics that might reconnect economics and politics in new forms of value and accounting.

Amid the pandemic, we have seen the domestic power of nation-states and the international power of central bankers working in tandem to stabilize the structures of financial capitalism—all in an effort to maintain the status quo ante. But we have also seen a dramatic display of the state's capacity to *demobilize* its economy in the name of protecting health. This offers a novel perspective from which to think about politics after neoliberalism and in the face of the Anthropocene. But the temptation to return to the old regime is immense. Who can say, then, that the project of neoliberalism has definitively run its course? Perhaps not even the pandemic has condemned it to the dustbin of history. But it is surely the challenge of the Anthropocene that provides the real trigger for thinking about a radically new way of conceiving of politics, rather than one that gives in to the temptations of the old.

AMONG THOSE MAJOR CHALLENGES are questions of value: what we owe nature, and what we owe to future generations. Such issues might embolden us to think anew about questions of reparations at the bar of ecological indebtedness, within which other forms of structural-historical injustice (such as racial slavery and patriarchal oppression) arose and continue to inform our present. The Anthropocene also questions conventional thinking about population, economic limits to growth, unevenly distributed forms of inequality, and the relationship between humans and other animals.

Much as with Beck's earlier treatment of ecological politics in an age of risk, these are problems that it is tempting to view through the prism of either a technocratic-legalist paradigm or a mitigation-adaptation perspective. The real challenge laid out by Beck, and through Anthropocene narratives and epistemologies today, is the thought that we might be better advised to drastically revise the established conventions and expectations around the terms we use to interrogate politics and economics, transfiguring both their histories and their values.

Rethinking the history and the ideas that shaped our politics into the present, we might be able to conceive of new and alternative forms of community. We might also, at the very least, go back to a more historically sensitive tradition of thinking about political economy, prevalent in the period before and during World War I, for hints about how to proceed to a politics beyond neoliberalism—particularly if that history can help us to see the longue durée of neoliberalism and its critics, rather than only its most recent forms. Consider antitrust progressives in the United States, historical political economists in Europe, and British political economists who worked out the relations between wealth, welfare, and the principles of taxation for negative externalities such as pollution: all offered ways of seeing the interconnections between politics, economics, history, and the environment that are more capacious and synthetic than anything modern neoliberalism and mainstream economics have to offer. All, as well, value complexity over predictive simplification.

Only by reconnecting questions of value to the properly embedded interrelationship between politics and economics can these visions become thinkable anew. The pandemic at least shows that it really is a very old question about the value of political economies or market societies that will have to bear the foundational weight of any future-oriented, progressive politics of the Anthropocene. Whether such rethinking might issue in the achievement of radical demands for forms of politics grounded in love, justice, and radical hope—or just follow the line of least resistance back to business as usual—remains to be seen. But one thing is certain: merely "following the science" will not get us anywhere close to a more progressive future, with or without the particular threats posed by this pandemic.

END CAPITALISM

Alexis Pauline Gumbs

excerpted from Undrowned: Black Feminist
Lessons from Marine Mammals

I WONDER IF we could outgrow rope. Braided with blood, a tangled legacy. Could we evolve past nets of capture, the intersecting technology of getting and keeping. I'm asking for a friend: Vaquita, the smallest living cetacean, whom EcoWatch says is days away from extinction because of the pervasive use of gillnets where she lives. And I'm asking for the North Atlantic right whale, also very close to extinction, whose major cause of death is getting caught in ropes used by large fishing vessels in her range. Or being stabbed by their propellers.

Neither of these species is having problems reproducing. North Atlantic right whales actually have a lot of reproductive sex and even more social sex just because.

Throughout the entire period of the slave trade, the North Atlantic right whale was targeted and hunted. But no one is hunting them now. The opposite, in fact: recently, Joe Howlett, a lobsterman and member of a team of people who risk their lives trying to untangle these whales from the ropes that kill them, died in the process.

Rather, the threat against the most critically endangered cetaceans on the planet (and most endangered marine mammals at this point) is an unintentional byproduct of fishing as usual. Could the large fishing boats in the Atlantic become mindful enough to sense and avoid an animal as big and slow moving as the North Atlantic right whale (which actually was named the "right whale" specifically because it was slow moving and large enough to easily hunt from large ships with the technology they had two hundred years ago)? To hear the industry tell it, it's expensive and difficult. They say the necessary technology is years if not decades away. In other words, it may be available after the North Atlantic right whale is already extinct.

And what about the gillnets in the tiny range of the vaquita? They are already illegal, and the fishers who use them are impoverished people without other economic options at this time.

So Alexis, are you saying that to save these animals we have to not only abolish the commercial fishing industry, which is one of the major food sources on the planet, but also abolish capitalism itself this week so no one needs to use an illegal gillnet or starve?

In a word? Yes.

But maybe you already know something about this. About how a deadly system doesn't have to seem like it's targeting you directly to kill you consistently. How, for example, long after the era of photographed lynchings where picnickers sliced off body parts and kept them as keepsakes, a system can still cut off parts of you daily, steal parts of yourself that you need. Maybe you think this is not about you (if so, that's a part that already went numb).

One female North Atlantic right whale was stabbed by a propeller as a baby and didn't die until fourteen years later when she was pregnant. As she expanded to hold life, her wound reopened, got infected, and killed her. Or think of Punctuation (this is what the researchers who have been studying this whale for forty years call her), a grandmother North Atlantic right whale who died in the summer of 2019. She had given birth eight times, survived entanglement five different times, and had scars from multiple boat strikes and propellers. And at least three of her children died from entanglement before she died. Maybe you know something about what it means to bear the constant wounding of a system that says it's about something else entirely. It might sound hollow to you too when you hear these deaths are not the point, that these deaths are just a byproduct that cannot be prevented for the sake of the system. Surely there must be some way to improve the system that already exists.

I don't think so. Where are the people who argue that commercial fishing is necessary for human life when the same economic system pollutes that exact food supply and raises carbon to levels that are killing fish off already? None of these things can be separated from each other. We are all entangled. And the fact that entanglement is a slow death doesn't make it any better; it in fact makes it more gruesome. And I mourn the parts of you that lost feeling today. I mourn the scars you will not notice until you have a reason to grow. I mourn the freedom you don't know because these ropes have been here longer than you have been and, big or small, you can't evade them.

If we don't do it, if we don't end capitalism this week, it is because we are entangled, a reality that will continue to wound us after the vaquita and the North Atlantic right whale disappear off the face of the Earth. So you don't have to save the whales, but at least take a look at the ropes. Acknowledge what has already been severed, the costs of this system as usual. At least take a moment to imagine how you would move if we weren't all caught up in this. Could we do that? I'm asking for myself. And if you can at all feel these last two sentences, then maybe it's not impossible: I love you. You deserve to be free.

THE STRIPED DOLPHIN (*Stenella coeruleoalba*) got sum to say. She's sick and tired. Of being sick and tired. She's been dealing with cycles of viruses that kill her species by the thousands and that are recurrent in the Atlantic, Pacific, and Mediterranean. A social, deep-water dolphin, the striped dolphin is vulnerable to cetacean disease outbreaks. If pilot whales have it, striped dolphins will get it. Researchers don't know the exact cause of the virus yet, but it killed a thousand dolphins in the Mediterranean Sea from 1990 to 1992, and came back in 2007 and again in 2019. One factor that I'm sure doesn't help is the pollution of the striped dolphin's habitat.

For example, right now in Greece, oil companies are scrambling to drill in marine-mammal protected areas, namely the deepest area of the Mediterranean Sea, where the striped dolphins live. A conservative (but not conservationist) Greek government that sees ocean drilling as the solution to all of Greece's economic problems is welcoming even the most reckless oil drillers to its shores. Of course, these politicians are not talking about the major potential costs of even a small oil spill in their region, not only for the marine mammals who live there, but also for the government itself and Greece's own tourism industry. I am writing this in solidarity with the Greek activists who are currently using music and community education to raise awareness and stop offshore drilling speculation.

Because I know what it feels like to be sick of systemic oppression and its cycles of extraction. The virus impacting these dolphins presses on their lungs, their brains. They struggle to breathe, they swim in strange circles. They end up far off course in a place that can't sustain them. Do you know something about this?

I too have been moving in circles, confused. I too have been struggling to breathe. I too have wondered how I got so far from what my body and spirit need. So many of us are dizzy and labored, bewildered and estranged. So what would I say if I were a striped dolphin?

I love you. And even on your sickest, saddest day, you deserve an ocean as blue as your name. You deserve a safety as deep as your need. You deserve food, community, school, and home. And you were not wrong to associate with your kindred. And you were not wrong to breathe loud about what you believed. And the dizziness you feel is justified. We are living in a world off course. And the pressure in your lungs is urgency. We have to learn the language of this air. We are sick of these tired cycles of economic vulnerability, resource grabs, and waste and harm spiraling down. We are ready to breathe differently. And evolve.

.

BAD ISLAND
illustrations by Stanley Donwood

ARTIST STANLEY DONWOOD is perhaps best known as a longtime collaborator of the band Radiohead, with whom he produces iconic album covers. Donwood's new, wordless graphic novel, *Bad Island*, reads like a medieval chapbook. It opens with a wild seascape, a distant island, a full moon. Gradually the island grows nearer until we land on a primeval wilderness, rich in vegetation and huge, strange beasts. Time passes and things do not go well for the wilderness. Civilization rises as towers of stone and metal and smoke choke the undergrowth and the creatures that once moved through it. This is not a happy story, and it will not have a happy ending. Working in his distinctive, monochromatic linocut style, Donwood offers a stark parable of environmental disaster and the end of civilization. The following four panels are excerpted from the book's middle.

CONTRIBUTORS

Ruby Bagwyn is a sophomore at Williams College.

Alyssa Battistoni is an Environmental Fellow at Harvard University and coauthor of *A Planet to Win: Why We Need a Green New Deal*.

Madison Condon is Associate Professor at Boston University School of Law, where she teaches Environmental Law and Corporations.

José A. Constantine is Assistant Professor of Geosciences at Williams College.

Stanley Donwood is a graphic designer and artist whose books include *Bad Island, Catacombs of Terror!, Slowly Downward, Small Thoughts,* and *There Will Be No Quiet*.

Erica X Eisen has published in *n+1*, the *Baffler,* the *Threepenny Review, AGNI,* and the *Washington Post*. She is an editor at *Hypocrite Reader*.

Catherine Coleman Flowers is founder of the Center for Rural Enterprise and Environmental Justice and author of *Waste: One Woman's Fight Against America's Dirty Secret*.

Jessica F. Green is Associate Professor of Political Science at the University of Toronto and author of *Rethinking Private Authority: Agents and Entrepreneurs in Global Environmental Governance*.

Alexis Pauline Gumbs is author of *Undrowned: Black Feminist Lessons from Marine Mammals* and *Dub: Finding Ceremony.*

Robert C. Hockett is Edward Cornell Professor of Law at Cornell Law School and author of *Financing the Green New Deal: A Plan of Action and Renewal.*

David McDermott Hughes is Professor of Anthropology at Rutgers University and author of *Energy Without Conscience: Oil, Climate Change, and Complicity.*

Duncan Kelly is Professor of Political Thought and Intellectual History at the University of Cambridge and author of *Politics and the Anthropocene.*

James A. Manigault-Bryant is Professor of Africana Studies at Williams College. His essays have been published in the *CLR James Journal*, the *Journal of Africana Religions*, and *Critical Sociology.*

Matto Mildenberger is Assistant Professor of Political Science at the University of California, Santa Barbara, and author of *Carbon Captured: How Business and Labor Control Climate Politics.*

Thea Riofrancos is Assistant Professor of Political Science at Providence College and author of *Resource Radicals: From Petro-Nationalism to Post-Extractivism in Ecuador.*

Charles Sabel is Maurice T. Moore Professor of Law and Social Science at Columbia Law School. His latest book on climate governance, coauthored with David G. Victor, is forthcoming with Princeton University Press in 2021.

Leah C. Stokes is Assistant Professor of Political Science at the University of California, Santa Barbara, author of *Short Circuiting Policy: Interest Groups and the Battle Over Clean Energy and Climate Policy in the American States*, and cohost of the podcast *A Matter of Degrees*.

David G. Victor is Professor of Industrial Organization and Technology Innovation at the University of California, San Diego, where he codirects the Deep Decarbonization Initiative, and adjunct Senior Fellow at the Brookings Institution. His latest book on climate governance, coauthored with Charles Sabel, is forthcoming with Princeton University Press in 2021.

David Wallace-Wells is Deputy Editor and climate columnist for *New York* and author of *The Uninhabitable Earth: Life After Warming*.